ON THE ROAD OF RECONCILIATION

John Morrow

On The Road Of Reconcilation
A Brief Memoir

the columba press

First published in 2003 by
the columba press
55A Spruce Avenue, Stillorgan Industrial Park, Blackrock, Co Dublin

Cover by Bill Bolger
Origination by Alan Evans
Printed in Ireland by ColourBooks Ltd, Dublin

ISBN 1 85607 411 0

Acknowledgements
I would like to thank and acknowledge help and advice from the Corrymeela Press,
in particular from Carrie Barkley and Peter Moss; thanks also to Angela Loudon for
typing the manuscript, to Alan Evans for preparing the material for printing, Helen
Baird for photographs, David Stevens for writing the foreword and my wife Shirley
for her ongoing support and keeping my feet on the ground!!

I wish to dedicate this brief memoir to the members and friends of the Corrymeela
Community, and to all who share our commitment to the work of reconciliation in
Ireland and throughout the world.

The publisher gratefully acknowledges the permission of the following to use
material in their copyright: Brian Frost for his poem Easter Rising 1988; SCM
Press for a quotation from John V. Taylor, *The Go-Between God*; Abingdon Press
for a quotation from *Exclusion and Embrace* by Miroslav Volf; Blackstaff Press for
a quotation from John Hewitt; Stainer and Bell Ltd, London, for a quotation from
Sydney Carter; Faber and Faber for a quotation from T. S. Eliot; Rider Publications
for a quotation from Desmond Tutu. New English Bible © Oxford University Press
and Cambridge University Press 1961, 1970.

Contents

FOREWORD

John Morrow's 'brief memoir' is entitled *On the Road of Reconciliation* with all the connotations of a journey. The book indeed represents John's journeyings.

His beginnings were on a family dairy farm close to Belfast in a strongly Presbyterian area. He is deeply rooted in Ulster Presbyterianism and exemplifies many of its virtues: integrity, a sense of fairness, a capacity for honest conversation, courage and persistence, an ability for hard work and a respect for words and their meaning. And, of course, like many Presbyterians he can be an awkward customer at times (and not only on a farm – see page 10). John's are not charismatic virtues but they are the virtues of a good companion on the Way.

John's journey has been a story of encounter with difference – all sorts of people pop up in this book – and a search for community – he was involved in Iona and he was in at the beginning of Glencree and Corrymeela. The journey has also taken John to different places: Edinburgh, Glasgow, Dublin, Seymour Hill, Belfast.

John became Leader of the Corrymeela Community after Ray Davey. First generation transitions in leadership are often difficult. It is a tribute to John and to Ray that the change took place so smoothly. Being Leader of such a heterogeneous group of people is not easy. There are many conflicting demands in holding us together. So, thank you, John, our companion. You have provided food for our journeys.

David Stevens
Easter 2002

CHAPTER 1

EARLY YEARS – FOUNDATIONS

'We shall not cease from exploration
And the end of all our exploring
Will be to arrive where we started
And know the place for the first time.'

TS Eliot
Little Gidding
Collected Poems 1909-62, (Faber and Faber)

My early years in the 30's were shaped by life on a family dairy farm in North Down close to the City of Belfast. Both of my parents came from families that had been rooted in the area for several generations. There was a strong sense of a way of life that had been going on for a long time and which was only beginning to change radically. Horsepower was literally 'horses' and it wasn't until the war period that tractors came in. Up to seven farm workers were needed to keep the show on the road, so we grew up in close contact with them and their families. The fact that they were both Catholic and Protestant was an important part of our early learning.

My father was outgoing and personable but given to strong outbursts of temper and panic when things were not going smoothly. My mother was in some ways shy but much more deeply at peace with herself, enabling her to ride the storms with amazing calm. Her religious faith had been sorely tested by the death of her younger brother and her father in quick succession and she had come through the crisis with a great depth and maturity. I was very close to my two brothers, one older and one younger, but there was a gap of ten years before my twin sisters were born. The need for all 'hands' on the farm drew us together in all kinds of tasks as well as our times at school and play.

I was also conscious of belonging to a wider community of relatives and neighbours, in the farming community and in the local church. The primary school had only two teachers in the early years, so it was possible to aspire to schoolwork with older or younger children depending on your interest or ability. Although we were far from being rich, and indeed the thirties were a difficult time for farming, I became very aware of the poverty of some of the families with which we shared at playtime on the farm or at school. These families were mainly Protestant because the Catholic farm workers were mostly single men.

The outbreak of war made a big impact on us as children. We heard the announcement on the radio after Sunday School. Soon we were fitted with gasmasks to carry each day to school in a cardboard box and war hero stories started to dominate our minds and imaginations. The presence of English soldiers began to impact on us as a family when my father offered them friendship in their time off and they taught us how to swim. When Belfast was bombed in May 1941 four bombs were dropped in our fields near the farmhouse and these included an unexploded landmine. We had to be temporarily evacuated whilst this was defused. I will never forget the scenes on the main roads on the morning after the first bombing. Thousands of women and children pushing prams, carts and whatever were streaming out of the city to find any place of refuge in the country (at the back of hedges, if necessary).

Shortly after this I changed school and attended Cabin Hill School which was open to dayboys of Campbell College. Whilst most of the boarders were evacuated to Portrush, the Main School had been taken over as a military hospital. 'Campbell' had a reputation as an elite 'public school' and some of my emotional reactions to its ethos were mixed. Catering as it did for the total life of boarders, especially after 1945, it had all-round facilities with many opportunities for different sports, interests clubs, etc. The approach to education was wholistic, so the academic side was encouraged but not overstressed. If anything, sport was king. However, its strong tradition of service in the forces and the prominent position of the Combined Cadet Corps gave it a militaristic and patriotic emphasis with which I was often uncomfortable. That, together with some tendency towards superiority and snobbery, was at times an embarrassment to me. However, we all owed a lot to the school and some of the staff made a big impression on our lives.

Because I did not want to lose touch with my local friends I struggled hard to maintain contact with church organisations like the B.B. and later on the Young Farmers' Club. However, school rugby tended to be a major preoccupation in our family and almost everything else was subservient to it! At vacation times, especially in the summer, we continued to be employed in various aspects of the life of the farm, mixing with the farm workers and getting to know them as friends. So we learnt all the skills from milking cows, feeding animals, stooking corn, setting potatoes, bottling milk, thinning turnips, calving cows, harnessing horses and eventually driving tractors. House decoration was badly missed out, much to my wife's later chagrin! Most of the skills I learnt are now redundant.

In the midst of all of this I became aware of some of the bigger issues that could cause conflict and found myself siding with the farm workers on issues of injustice – to the dismay of my father. I also came to respect the different gifts of Catholic and Protestant and to see through some of the popular prejudical myths, as for example, timekeeping. Protestant workers were regarded as good timekeepers, Catholics were not. However, on closer examination the situation was something like this. Protestant workers mostly started on time but they were usually equally strict about when they finished. Catholic workers may have sometimes started late but they were more open to working on after 'quitting time' if a job needed to be finished. So in the end the amount of work done was not significantly different.

On reflection, this period of my life was one where I was fortunate enough to have a deep sense of belonging, arising out of the ongoing participation in the life of a family farm. The opportunity to meet people across a wide spectrum of social and religious backgrounds gave me an openness to others and a capacity to cooperate with them in order to complete the tasks which had to be done. Of course we complained at times and longed to be free from the chores, but we gained so much through living and sharing together in a life of real community.

I was only beginning to be aware of the depth of division in our society and of some of the injustices that were part of it, but foundations were being laid and relationships built which would be of tremendous support to me in the days ahead. Having an older brother who took a lot of responsibility probably allowed me the luxury to concentrate on academic work and to prepare myself for university. A tendency towards accident-proneness was probably a sign that I wasn't very good, at times, at looking after my own safety.

In later years, reflecting on these early days, I realise that some of the close bonding was the result of scapegoating my father, ridiculing him and making him the butt of family humour. In truth he set himself up for this role, but I can now see that he wasn't any more eccentric or abnormal than many others. In the process we probably failed to recognise some of his strengths and our own flaws. Fortunately my mother was wise enough to see beyond our attempts to ridicule him and to trust her own intuitive wisdom. She had the capacity to accept him as he was, in spite of some of the pain he imposed on her; she genuinely loved him and was hopelessly bereft when he died.

My father was a horse-lover with every bone in his body and without doubt, next to his family, his greatest joy was to be with them day and night. Feeding and grooming, breaking and training, foaling and nurturing, showing and racing and, above all, treating their ailments. He considered himself an amateur vet and was the supreme advocate of TCP as a 'cure-all' for everything, including broken brush shafts. Even the family were forced to gargle TCP drinks throughout the winter to keep our throats right. The house reeked of it. It also created some serious difficulties when my younger brother, Terence, became a vet! He poured scorn on some of the new-fangled ideas of the veterinary colleges.

In some ways Terence fulfilled what my father would have wished for himself (to be a vet) but didn't get the chance. I think he would have made a better vet than a farmer. Even though I was often bored to tears by his endless stories of 'form' and 'breeding' I now realise the encyclopaedic knowledge that he had on the world of thoroughbreds. His father (my grandfather) had been a horse dealer as well as a farmer and had travelled the length and breadth of Ireland to sell horses for England. At that time of course the main market was for horse transport. This tradition of contact with all of the island of Ireland was very much alive in our family. My grandfather spent most of his days in our home during my childhood, returning only in the evening to his own house nearby. Although my father was not politically very 'up front' it is clear that my grandfather had been and it gradually dawned on me that he had been a strong supporter of Home Rule. As a result, he had a good deal of scorn for the great white building on the Holywood Hills opposite us, i.e. the Stormont Parliament. He called it 'a great white elephant'.

Another sign of the tradition was the daily paper that was delivered – *The Northern Whig* – and it was a long time before I saw a copy of the *Belfast Newsletter*, never mind the *Telegraph* or the *Irish News*. In retrospect it is clear that a lot of this rubbed off on me subconsciously. I have never had a sense of the South of Ireland as alien territory in the way that many unionists feel. Indeed, for a significant period, my father's brother lived in Dublin and was married to a woman from the Midlands. Even my knowledge of Southern geography was often assisted by the names of racecourses like Navan, Naas, Clonmel, Galway, The Curragh and Fairyhouse. I have always had a difficulty about defining my nationality and feel confidently both British and Irish.

I do recognise the Ulster/Scots aspect too and that was probably strongest in my mother's family (Watson). My uncle Robert quoted the appropriate phrase from Rabbie Burns at every opportunity and my maternal grandmother had many a pithy phrase. When I later spent time in Scotland both in study and work I felt no sense of alienation at all and at times a deep sense that I was recovering deep roots. The strong Presbyterian connections make the link even more natural and intuitive, but more about that later.

My mother and father had no secondary education but my mother was a natural reader with a deeply thoughtful disposition. All the old classics of literature were on our shelves and George Eliot was a special favourite. Reading and listening to radio plays were a normal part of our lives. Above all she was a deeply spiritual person with a profound understanding of the central doctrines of the faith and their practical meaning in daily life. At one stage in my life I put this to the test by ridiculing some of her pre-scientific presuppositions but I later realised that although I deluded myself that I had won the arguments, I knew in my heart that she possessed something very precious which I lacked. Her brother became an agricultural missionary in India and she supported him and his family through all the stresses and strains of their times of separation. Her closest friend was also a GA missionary and I suspect she might have been one if circumstances had been different.

At the end of school I wrestled with various possibilities but in the end I succeeded in winning an agricultural scholarship to study at Queen's, so a new stage in my life began.

CHAPTER 2

STUDENT YEARS – CHALLENGE AND VISION

'Catch the Bird of Heaven, lock him in a cage of gold
Look again tomorrow and he will be gone.

Ah the Bird of Heaven! Follow where the Bird has gone
If you want to find him, keep on travelling on.

Lock him in religion. Gold and frankincense and myrrh
Carry to his prison but he will be gone.

Temple made of marble, beak and feather made of gold,
Bell and book and candle, but he will be gone.

Bell and book and candle cannot hold him any more
Still the Bird is flying as he did before.

Ah the Bird of Heaven! Follow where the Bird has gone
If you want to find him, keep on travelling on.'

Sydney Carter

When I arrived at Queen's Students Union on the first day of Freshers' Week I was accosted by a senior student called Craig Clements who invited me to become a member of the Student Christian Movement (SCM). With some hesitation I decided to give this a try and I found it at first a mind-stretching and disturbing experience. Two experiences stand out in my mind. The first was a study group I attended on the theme of Marxism and Christianity that was so far above my head that I seriously wondered whether I would ever return. The older students in the group (some of whom were ex-service) were intellectually so far ahead of me that I daren't speak a word in case I exposed my invincible ignorance. The second was a meeting for prayer that was led by Anglicans and most of those present seemed to be Anglicans as well. Liturgical type prayers were used and most people knelt and although I remained in my usual Presbyterian hunched position, I came away with the feeling that I was being pressurised to conform. Of course this was entirely within my head and was simply an expression of my own insecurity and lack of self-confidence.

However, these two experiences proved to be symbolic of the beginnings of two major journeys in my life. The intellectual journey that was part of the whole experience of university life began to raise issues that threatened the whole basis of my religious worldview. This was particularly poignant in the area of science and the latest books by Fred Hoyle were producing vigorous debate amongst some of my classmates. Side by side with the SCM was a more conservative society called the Christian Union that was preoccupied with the need to nurture sound orthodox doctrine and to protect students from exposure to the heresies of liberal thought and the demonic dangers of atheism. I thank God for the SCM that refused to cosset me from these upsetting currents of thought but took up the challenge to wrestle with the issues in order to fashion a faith that had integrity. It was a Society that welcomed honest doubt and was patiently open to work through the vexed questions of our time. It did not give me easy answers but it prepared me for the real world and launched me on a journey that continues to this day as new frontiers open before us at the beginning of a new millennium.

The second journey was, of course, the ecumenical journey and was interwoven with the first, but it was only as a student that I began to encounter, in depth, traditions of the faith other than my own homespun Presbyterianism. It is probably difficult for people to understand that the part of North Down in which I lived was so intensely Presbyterian, and my family and close friends were all so linked with it, that I had almost as little awareness of Anglicanism as I had of Roman Catholicism. The process of breaking out of one's familiar culture and recognising a common faith, expressed in a different way, is both upsetting and enriching. It was the beginning of a journey that was to become far more significant for me than I ever guessed at that time.

Life at university had many dimensions of course, including sport and study and my natural interest in science and agriculture gave me enough motivation to keep abreast of the course. Oddly enough, although I was vaguely aware of the existence of Ray Davey and the Presbyterian Centre, I did not make a strong connection there until a later stage in my course. I think it was at a point when I was finding it difficult to reconcile the various conflicting 'worldviews' with which I was being assaulted that I found his pastoral resource available to me in the form of a patient listener. With great gentleness and skill he put before me a series of books by writers like John Baillie, William Temple and Brian Green, etc. which nurtured my faith through periods of doubt and black despair. Ray's interest in 'Community' and his development of an environment in which trusting relationships could grow was an important balance to the intellectual robustness of the SCM. Two of Ray's great innovations were the development of 'houseparties' held at Castlerock and the planning of European visits that were not just holidays but opportunities to encounter frontier movements in Christian renewal and think-tanks on the reconstruction of Europe after the devastation of World War II.

Ray's recent experience as a youth worker and a prisoner of war had given him a breadth and a depth of spirituality and humanity that enabled him to sow seeds in our growing minds. It was his links with George MacLeod of the Iona Community that proved to be of greatest significance for the next stage in my journey. I first met George when he came to speak to a student audience at Queen's (through Ray's invitation). There was something arresting about his presence and something robust about his humanity that held my attention. He spoke with an empathy for the gambler, the alcoholic, the person who wanted 'life' with a capital L, even if they were hopelessly looking for it in the wrong place. I remember he reiterated that text in John's gospel, 'I have come that they shall have life and have it more abundantly' and then he said that sometimes the church has turned it into 'moribundantly'. The gospel, he said, was about life here and now in all its fullness. In so many Christian presentations I had often detected an 'anti-life' dimension. The gospel call to self-denial seemed to be interpreted in a life-denying way. The negatives had been emphasised rather than the offer of real life. George knew that self-giving was at the heart of the gospel but he understood the paradox of 'losing our life in order to find it'.

It took some time before I followed up this new track and made my way to Iona, but in retrospect I can see that there was a certain inevitability about it. However, in the meantime, I completed my undergraduate studies in Agriculture and Science and took up a research fellowship in the Plant Breeding Department of the Ministry of Agriculture based at Loughgall in Co Armagh. Living amongst the apple trees of Armagh with a local landlady who cooked every form of apple-based food imaginable, I discovered that here is one form of food that I can take in any form *ad infinitum*. My love of apple tart and blackberry and apple pudding has been life long!

I finally made a visit to join an Iona Youth Camp in the summer of 1953 and began to learn something of the whole Iona story and the movement that had grown out of it. The details of that story are now widely available to anyone who is interested and I have written about its influence on the Corrymeela Community elsewhere. Suffice to say George MacLeod was a minister of the Church of Scotland in the industrial parish of Govan Glasgow in the 30s. He had previously fought in World War I and was awarded the MC but had later become a pacifist. In his ministry in Glasgow during the hungry 30s he became increasingly aware of a yawning gulf between the church and the unemployed shipyard workers and their families in the parish.

To cut a long story short, after setting up a number of projects for the unemployed and drawing his congregation into a creative encounter with the poor, he was eventually led to set up a project in Christian renewal based on the island of Iona. Iona has had a unique history in the life of Scotland and the story of Christianity. Beginning with the 6th-century Celtic period it became the base from which Columcille (or Columba) from Derry in Northern Ireland launched his mission to Scotland and eventually Northern England. In the 12th century it was the base of a Benedictine Abbey that later fell into ruins after the closing of monasteries at the time of the Reformation. So, in a way, the island embodied many different phases of the life of the Christian Church. At the turn of the century the abbey church was rebuilt by the Church of Scotland but the remainder of the monastery was still in ruins.

With his genius for symbolism George noticed that the church had rebuilt the 'religious' bit of the abbey and neglected the living and working places, i.e.

the kitchens, refectory, bedrooms, chapter house, etc. He saw this as depicting what was happening to the church as a whole. He wanted to reintegrate the gospel with the whole of life, to recover all its dimensions and to proclaim its message of healing and wholeness. 'Whole' salvation instead of 'soul' salvation. To start the process he brought together a group of craftsmen and ordinands asking them to go to an island (where there was no easy escape) to re-build the abbey buildings and in the process learn how to communicate with each other and how to communicate the gospel.

All of this had now led to a broadly-based movement known as the Iona Community that became involved in all the frontier situations of mission amongst youth, in the parishes of the new housing schemes of Scotland, in industrial mission and in work overseas in India, Southern Africa, etc. It was about holding together faith and life, work and worship, prayer and politics, body and spirit; about the renewal of the church and the transformation of people and society.

My experience as a youth camper further whetted my appetite for this new vision of the church which was drawing ecumenically on all the different traditions of our history, yet at the same time, exposing itself to a robust encounter with all the disturbing realities of the world today. Inevitably, peacemaking was at the centre of this and the challenges of nuclear war, economic injustice and the vicious racism in the world were at the forefront of the Community's witness. One way of becoming linked with the movement was to become a 'Youth Associate' so I signed up to see what this would mean. This was probably the first time I was given a structure for daily prayer, Bible study and active discipleship, in spite of all the other church contacts that I had experienced. I was aware of course of the more pietistic patterns of evangelical groups but had kept clear of them because they were 'religious' in a way that made me feel uncomfortable. Now I had a similar discipline but one that was focused on the issues of our time and the social as well as personal challenges. The Bible was being interpreted in a prophetic way that enabled me to see the realities of injustice and the sources of conflict in a new way. God was alive and at work in the midst of it all, if only we had the eyes to see and the ears to listen. It was a rediscovery of the 'word made flesh' through the humanity of Jesus, without which his 'divinity' only placed him in a stained glass window. As MacLeod put it, 'Jesus Christ was crucified on a cross between two thieves, not on an altar between two candlesticks.'

This new commitment in my life left me a bit uncertain about the current direction of my career and I began to explore possible ways of serving overseas in some capacity, doing agricultural research for developing countries. For some reason all my efforts to find such a position came to nothing and my mind began to turn to the work of renewing the church in Ireland along the lines that Iona were pursuing. Because I had been infected by a vision of the church as the whole people of God, I was not yet convinced that ordination to the ministry was my calling. But the more I wrestled with the idea the more I became convinced that I needed to train myself in theology by one method or another. In the end, although unsure if I would necessarily go for ordination, I decided to sign up on the course for the ministry in the Presbyterian Church in Ireland and in 1955 I began my studies at the Assembly's College in Belfast.

The shock I received in my first year at the college was almost enough to disillusion me completely with church and Christianity. I found myself amongst a group of students who were in a state of paranoia about any critical evaluation of the Bible and who were being held in the grip of a doctrinaire fundamentalism with the aid of senior students acting like a KGB! Fortunately there were a few exceptions who enabled me to retain my sanity and one good friend advised me to transfer to Edinburgh at the end of the first year. Before that I decided to join an Iona Community Summer Scheme. With my Iona connections this seemed a wise move but I signed on at New College, University of Edinburgh in September 1956. It was a good decision.

The Iona Community Scheme which I joined in the summer of 1956 involved working in industry for three months and I was placed in Alexander Stephen's shipyard in Glasgow. This was an exposure to the daily life of an industrial labourer at the 'coalface'. I had often travelled in the bus to Belfast with shipyard workers as I made my way to university, but it was just another world that I observed from a distance. Now it was part of my daily life and the impact was traumatic. As a farmer's son I was not immune from contact with rough language, but nothing could have prepared me for the avalanche of four letter Anglo Saxon words used as verb, noun, adjectives in an endless stream.

The second impact was that of the danger with which men lived – long before the strict regulations about hard hats had come in. Quite frequently during my time men fell from great heights in the hull of the ship and after a great horn sounded we all waited in silence as a crane was lowered to lift the injured (or dead man). On one occasion I was asked to climb a narrow ladder to the top of a mast laden with radar equipment. No account was taken of my plea that I had no head for heights! The moral dilemmas that arose when one worked as part of a squad were excruciating. In effect, the boss had to do a deal with the squad about the number of jobs that were acceptable and we regularly took breaks of an hour when the leader refused to take on any more work. At times I was ordered to hide in the funnel so that the boss would not be able to find us. Most of the jobs required a group so it was impossible to offer to work on one's own. On the other hand, my sympathy for the men was often aroused by the way they were treated and unvalued. The main injury I received was to scald my finger making the tea!

At the end of our period of work we spent a week on Iona reflecting on our experiences and what it means to be the church in the daily life of industry. To help us in this we had industrial chaplains, trade union officials and others. It was an enlightening and sobering experience that gave me a lifelong empathy with the industrial workers I met in later parts of my ministry.

Arriving in Edinburgh in September 1956, I was enthralled by the city in terms of its history and architecture. Life in the New College residence, along with students from Scotland and many other nations, was the most educative experience I had yet received. In addition, I met several students who were touched by the Iona vision and I connected with the local branch of the 'Youth Associates'. It was as a result of this that I met the girl who was later to become my wife – at a Youth Associates' Haggis Party.

Throughout my student years I had been developing a gradual interest in politics, and at Queen's I had become linked with the Ulster Liberal Association. When I took the entrance scholarship exam in Edinburgh the Suez crisis was upon us and I wrote a critique of British policy in one of my answers. This particular event led to one of the only serious rows I ever had with my older brother (now at home running the farm) who was an ardent supporter of Anthony Eden. My growing contacts with Iona were leading me further to the left and into sympathy with the Labour Party. Something of my earlier 'trade union' role with the farm workers was stirring in my breast as I became more and more aware of the injustices all around me.

My studies at New College were stimulating and I was free from all the restraints of the 'evangelical police force'. Tom Torrance, John McIntyre, James Stewart and James Barr all made their distinctive influence felt as I opened myself to reflect on the various dimensions of the gospel. It was with real regret that I returned to Belfast to complete my third year for I did not have the financial resources to transfer my course completely to Edinburgh. But it was the Iona 'bug' which had infected me and I knew that I would be keeping this connection no matter what.

At the end of the term at Edinburgh 1957 I began to make preparations to lead Youth Camps on Iona during the month of August. It was no coincidence that Shirley, my wife to be, was acting as a cook at another similar camp on the island. It was an exhausting but enjoyable experience that included one period when the island was storm bound and people could neither arrive or leave. I have never seen mountainous seas like it and we almost ran out of food to feed the hungry campers. Several boatmen were drowned that year at Craignure on the island of Mull. Strangely, I have never experienced the beauty of these Western Hebridean Isles so deeply as in the midst of that storm. It was raw nature in its most awesome mood.

I returned to Belfast to complete my theological course, now certain in my mind that I would become a full member of the Iona Community and enter their training scheme on Iona the following July. The year was difficult for obvious reasons. My relationship with Shirley, who lived in Edinburgh and was completing her course in dentistry, was put to the test of separation, apart from vacation contacts at Youth Associate events, etc. Also, I was missing the stimulus of living in New College Residence and the theological openness of that intellectual climate. One compensation was that I began to get to know the elderly Principal Davey at the College and to realise what a fund of knowledge he had on every subject from literature to philosophy and theology. I also had an enjoyable experience as a student assistant at St John's, Newtownbreda where there was a large and lively youth movement and a minister with a deep humanity and theological openness.

In June 1958, after being licensed for the Ministry of The Presbyterian Church in Ireland, I returned to Scotland to begin my period of training with the Iona Community. This began with a three-month stint on the island, working with craftsmen on the rebuilding of Iona Abbey. On alternate days we met with staff and members of the Community to reflect on different aspects of the Iona vision and its outworking in different parts of Scotland and the wider world. We also shared responsibility for leading the daily liturgies and in a common life that involved us in preparation of meals and daily chores as well as the rebuilding. There were ten of us, all men and mostly Church of Scotland ordinands, but including an Australian, an Englishman and myself. At this stage the Community membership was exclusively male and mostly clergy, but this changed significantly in later years. The only lay members at this time were the craftsmen, some of whom were Highlanders and others from Glasgow or Edinburgh.

I was assigned the task of working on the cloisters with a stonemason from Dunblane. After three weeks hard work we had reconstructed the first arch. To my horror I realised the stonemason was not satisfied that it was 'straight' and we were obliged to pull it down and start all over again. It was a lesson in patience and an insight into the mind of a stonemason who saw his work as longlasting and his reputation at stake. There were other lessons to be learnt in building the walls. 'Never throw a stone down, there's always a place for it if you wait!' All in all there was a 'down to earthness' in these relationships with the craftsmen that brought me back to my earlier experiences with the farmworkers. Unless the Christian faith could take root here, it could not pass the test of reality. Unless the gospel had a common language that transcended our differing backgrounds, its truth and authenticity was under question.

The reflective periods provided us with a chance to develop our relationships as a team and also to meet older members of the Community who were working in new housing schemes, as chaplains in industry or on furlough from India or Southern Africa. Ralph Morton, Deputy Leader of the Community, took responsibility for arranging our programme and made his own unique contribution arising out of many years service in China. During the Community Week, the whole Community gathered on the island and we had a chance to meet the full range of members and hear reports of the work they were doing in their own localities.

Slowly and surely the distinctive Iona theology was becoming lodged in our minds and hearts. The robust image of Christ at the heart of this cut through some of the sentimental images of my childhood. It was a life-affirming creed focused on 'wholeness' as the dominant image for salvation. The weekly Healing Service sought to recover the intimate connection between body and spirit and between the healing of the individual and the healing of community.

Prayer and politics were intimately connected as we reflected on the injustices of society, the sins of racism and the challenges of non-violence in the face of nuclear escalation. How does the church enable real community to come into existence in the deserts of industry or impersonal housing schemes? But at the heart of it all was the need for deep personal commitment to Christ. The social and personal gospel were held together in creative tension. The prophetic books of the Bible came alive with a new freshness. The increasing irrelevance of denominations and the contradictions of church disunity as a counter witness in a divided world, pointed to the need to recover the central message of the gospel in terms of reconciliation and peacemaking.

Some of the contradictions of this vision were beginning to pose questions for the Community itself in terms of its all-male membership and low ratio of lay members. George MacLeod was so convinced of the need to re-train the clergy that he was reluctant to move on these other frontiers in case the focus of the experiment was lost. However, it was not possible for him to hold out much longer as the number of women associated with the Community in a wider sense was growing.

The next stage of training began with a two-year placement in a Church of Scotland parish where the Minister in Charge was a member of the Community. I was sent to work with David Millar at Richmond Cragmillar in Edinburgh.

CHAPTER 3

PARISH MINISTRY – BUILDING COMMUNITY

'You coasted along
to larger houses, gadgets, more machines,
to golf and weekend bungalows,
caravans when the children were small,
the Mediterranean, later, with the wife …

When that noisy preacher started,
He seemed old-fashioned, a survival.
Later you remarked on his vehemence,
A bit on the rough side.
But you said, admit,you said in the club,
"you know there's something in what he says"'.

From The Coasters
The Selected John Hewitt
(Blackstaff 1981)

Richmond Cragmillar Parish was in the Niddrie Mains District of SE Edinburgh and was made up of very low quality 'council housing'. The district suffered from serious neglect and the social problems of the area were aggravated by a policy of housing ex-prisoners in one street so that the police could keep an eye on them. These people were at the bottom of the pile in Edinburgh society and many of them had their lives scarred by violence, unemployment, family break-up, poverty and low social esteem. The church was a small nucleus of people in a sea of non-churchgoing.

The aim of almost anyone who had any ability or ambition was to get out of the district so that leadership, scarce as it was, kept being eroded. There were of course those whose lives were permanently rooted there and amongst them a number of saintly people who were devoted to caring for their neighbours. The quality and dedication of their practical witness will remain in my memory always. In addition to pastoral visitation, I gave some time to youth work and found myself embroiled in conflict with the Church Officer who saw his main function as preserving the property from the dangers of exposure to the 'wild youth of the district'.

The warm support of David and Jean Miller (minister and minister's wife) made the experience tolerable but it was a devastating exposure to the gulf between the church and working class society in Scotland. Shirley, my wife to be, bravely supported me and for a period we lived in a council house in the parish after we were married, much to the horror of my mother-in-law who knew only of the estate from its reputation in the daily crime record of the newspapers. In July of 1960 we moved back to Ireland to share responsibility for two new linked congregations in two new housing estates (Seymour Hill and Lambeg) with the Rev Alec Watson.

We took up residence at the rear of the estate in a small upstairs flat with two bedrooms. Two of our children were born there and it provided a good base from which to connect with all the new families moving into the area. Indeed my early pastoral work was often combined with helping people carry furniture into their houses, after which I might tentatively ask the question, 'Are you by any chance Presbyterian?' to which the reply was sometimes, 'After all your help I think I'd better be one!'

With so many families moving in from so many different places, many from inner city Belfast, others from Lisburn and Dunmurry and many from rural areas, the obvious challenge was 'How can we build a community here?' A beautiful new church had just been built before we arrived and two other churches, Methodist and Church of Ireland, were also becoming established. I couldn't help but feel that our denominational identities were in the process of dividing the community rather than uniting it. We did explore the possibility of sharing ancillary buildings for social, recreational and community activities but found ourselves blocked due to the lack of confidence by our respective church authorities and the fear that such sharing could create dangerous legal wrangles and could cause more trouble than it was worth. So the advice was effectively to build our own empires and co-operate where it was appropriate. In fairness there had been a number of serious experiments in sharing, mainly between Methodist and Presbyterian churches, but it was not encouraged in this instance.

In practice we did manage to co-operate in a number of areas, i.e. with a joint Methodist/Presbyterian BB, shared Youth Fellowship meetings, etc. I also found a welcome support from my Church of Ireland colleague in promoting an ecumenical spirit and in resisting the rising influence of anti-Catholicism that was emanating from a local Free Presbyterian church. Indeed, we were probably amongst the first places where this bitter spirit, which was to become a significant factor in our troubles, had its public manifestation.

It happened something like this. The Rev Ian Paisley and some of his cohorts were beginning to make their presence felt in ways that were intimidating to anyone who wished to promote better relationships and understanding between Protestants and Catholics. This sometimes took the form of standing outside those churches where a minister had invited a priest to speak to his Youth Fellowship. I decided to write a letter to the *Belfast Telegraph* highlighting this form of intimidation and comparing it to the activities of Fascists. This was taken up by the Free Presbyterian Church in an article in the *Protestant Telegraph* and part of my letter was reprinted as a leaflet and distributed into every house in the Dunmurry and Seymour Hill district. The article was a grave distortion of what I said and it had a large type heading: 'Minister says Protestants are fascists, Catholics are Christians.'

It was with some trepidation that I entered the pulpit the following Sunday when I made a brief statement alerting the congregation to the distortion of my letter but offering to meet with anyone who wished to have clarification. At the end of the whole episode two or three members did decide to leave the congregation but the vast majority refused to rise to the bait. I was greatly encouraged during this episode by a personal letter from the Editor of the *Belfast Telegraph*, John E Sayers, thanking me for my letter and saying how important he felt it to be to counter this dangerous sectarian trend.

This incident and many others like it took place in the context of a time of significant change and reaction to change which began to happen throughout the sixties and which permeated the atmosphere of our whole period at Kilmakee (Seymour Hill). The Vatican II Council had created a new atmosphere of dialogue and openness in the Roman Catholic Church leading to opportunities for joint Bible study and other meetings, especially amongst a group of ecumenical clergy. I was involved in those early meetings initiated by Professor James Haire and Father Michael Hurley, that took place in St Malachy's College.

On the wider political front, Captain Terence O'Neill had met with Sean Lemass and was attempting to build a more cordial approach to North-South co-operation on the island. He also began to make gestures of friendship to the Roman Catholic community and attempted to thaw some of the cold-war attitudes that were still widespread in the province. The climate of change led eventually to the birth of the Civil Rights Movement in the later 60s, but long before that the loyalist reaction to these changes was emerging under the leadership of the Rev Ian Paisley.

It was during this period too that I became involved in the initiative that led to the formation of the Corrymeela Community. There were many factors that influenced the group of people who came together in 1964, including the atmosphere of change referred to above. Some of the group were former students who had retained their links with Ray Davey, the QUB Presbyterian Chaplain. Others were individuals like Alec Watson who, like myself, had been strongly influenced by the Iona Community, but the core of the group were current students at Queen's who had been exploring the concept of Christian Community as a result of visits to various renewal centres in Britain and Europe.

We were concerned about the divisions in church and society. We were also concerned about the need to relate faith and life together in a realistic way that would enable Christian lay members to fulfil their vocation in the church and in the world. We had a conviction that the central theme of the gospel was 'reconciliation' and that we were being called to put this conviction to the test in practical ways. We realised that this was going to involve us going on new journeys, not only in outreach, but also inwardly to the heart of our faith and to a rediscovery of the meaning of the conviction that 'God was in Christ reconciling the world to himself' and calling us to be servants of reconciliation.

As we met fortnightly to share our ideas around a meal, and to seek God's guidance in prayer and worship, we were drawn to express our vision in the form of a 'Centre for meeting' which would be an 'Open Village' – open to all. All of this crystallised when the Corrymeela Holiday Fellowship Centre near Ballycastle came on the market and we had the chance to root a thousand ideas in one concrete project. Because the building was in a dilapidated condition, it provided a challenge to bring together all the energy and idealism of youth across our divides to begin to make the place habitable, through numerous workcamps. At the same time we developed the concept of a dispersed community of members who shared the vision of the Centre and who saw it as a resource and an inspiration for their life and work in their local situations.

This was immediately relevant to me as a parish minister in Kilmakee. It gave me a sense of participation in the wider mission of church and society and it was a practical resource for my ministry. After the Centre was opened for use in October 1965 I was one of the first to bring a congregational group for a weekend community building exercise. The idea of the workcamps too had a special significance for us back at Kilmakee as we pondered how to provide facilities for the growing number of families. The multi-purpose use of the church building was putting a strain on the fabric and there was a growing demand for a hall that could supply additional facilities. However, the families were all under financial strain in rented housing with very moderate incomes and the only possible way to tackle this was by the use of the skills of the members themselves.

Although this project proved to be a stern test of the staying power of the core group of men who committed themselves, it did succeed in giving many of them a sense of 'ownership' and belonging that was a significant step in the building of 'real community'. There were many hiccups on the way that tested us to the limit. A decision by our appointed clerk of works to relay the floor after discovering that it was not level was accepted with a degree of humility that I could not have taken for granted. Grace was surely somewhere at work and a possible souring of relationships just didn't happen. I was reduced at times to desperation as I sought for helpers to spread ready-mix concrete before it became an unplanned statue. Some tasks and all materials had to be paid for, so a team of visitors led by Peggy Dunlop, one of our key leaders, faithfully called at the houses of all who agreed to give their contribution every Friday evening. When the project ended many complained about the loss of the regular visits that had led to many new friendships. In these simple ways a new community was built, brick by brick.

Towards the end of this project I received an unexpected invitation to return to Scotland as chaplain to overseas students in Glasgow. It was a difficult decision. I was a bit exhausted by all the efforts to build a new congregation but my close involvement with Corrymeela made it hard to leave Ulster at a time pregnant with possibilities and dangers. On the other hand, our Scottish connections with the Iona Community and Shirley's homeland made it seem the right kind of change that could stimulate and challenge us to cross the frontiers of race and religion and learn more about the wider mission of the church in a changing world.

After much prayer and reflection we decided to accept the invitation and we prepared to move to Glasgow at Easter 1967.

CHAPTER 4

SCOTLAND REVISITED

CROSSING BOUNDARIES

'This tired disillusioned, cynical world hurting so frequently and so grievously,
has been intrigued by a process that holds out considerable hope in the midst
of much that negates hope. People in different places where I have visited and
where I have spoken about the Truth and Reconciliation Commission process
see in this flawed attempt a beacon of hope, a possible paradigm for dealing
with situations where violence, conflict, turmoil and sectional strife have
seemed endemic, conflicts that take place not between warring nations but
within the same nation. At the end of their conflicts, the warring groups in
Northern Ireland, the Balkans, the Middle East, Sri Lanka, Burma,
Afghanistan, Angola, the Sudan, the two Congos and elsewhere are going to
have to sit down together to determine how they will be able to live together
amicably, how they might have a shared future devoid of strife, given the
bloody past they have recently lived through. They see more than just a
glimmer of hope in what we have attempted in South Africa.
God does have a sense of humour. Who in their right mind could ever have
imagined South Africa to be an example of anything but awfulness?'

Desmond Tutu
No Future without Forgiveness
(Rider 1999)

The invitation to work in Glasgow had come to us from David Millar with
whom I had worked previously in Edinburgh. He was now the University
Chaplain in Glasgow and a key member of the Ecumenical Committee that
made the appointment. This was therefore of great help to us in the settling
in process as we moved our young family into a large upstairs flat in
Dowanhill Street. It was one of the coldest Aprils of the century and we

wondered whether we had moved to Iceland since the large flat was without central heating, apart from two storage heaters in the hall.

Glasgow is perhaps the most friendly city I have ever lived in, much more so than Edinburgh, perhaps because it has been a place through which so many people have passed on the way to somewhere else. The Highland Clearances led to many people passing through on the way to Canada and some stayed. The Irish came in large numbers after the famine and more recently the Pakistanis and many others, including a significant Jewish Community. On the other hand, in 1967 before the facelift of the 70s and 80s, the black buildings and the dark autumn and winter days made it far from attractive to students from sunny Asia and Africa.

There were approximately 1,500 students from up to 70 different countries studying at the two universities and the many other colleges and hospitals in the city. The larger groups came from countries such as Nigeria, Pakistan and India but there were many from other parts of Africa, Cyprus, Hong Kong, Singapore, North and South America and Europe, as well as from places that stretched my knowledge of geography to the limit – like obscure West Indian islands and Indian Ocean islands like Mauritius.

Sixty per cent of them were from Hindu, Muslim, Sikh faiths and the forty per cent Christian were from every tradition, Orthodox, Roman Catholic and Protestant of various hues. As I began to build links with them and visit them in the dingy tenements and flats that they occupied, I soon began to realise that the qualification for this job was 'a stomach of steel'. Again and again students wished to honour me with their favourite dish – home-cooked! It could be anything from hot curry to boiled eyes and to refuse to partake was to lose all possible hope of establishing any relationship. My task, in so far as it could be defined, was to welcome these strangers in the name of the Church of Jesus Christ and to provide opportunities for them to meet with people from the local community. But of course that was only a starting point for an encounter across so many cultural, racial and religious boundaries that involved me with many aspects of their lives in ways I could never have suspected. If ever there was a good training ground for a later ministry of reconciliation, this was it.

Our flat had one large room that provided a base for open house hospitality and our family greatly benefited from this opportunity to meet such a varied selection of the human race. Our eldest son's hobby of collecting travel brochures for imaginary journeys was given some concrete focus by these weekly encounters. Many of the students, coming from large families, enjoyed the friendship of the children more than anything and it helped them to feel at home. On one famous occasion when my daughter Alison was sitting on the knee of a West Indian nurse she began pummel her leg to get attention. I heard myself shout at her, 'Stop! you'll have Mamita black and blue!', before I realised what I was saying. Alison replied with the words 'but dad she is black and blue!' Mamita laughed good-naturedly at my words!

In a job like this the whole area of race relations was an inevitable part of the work and I had some involvement with anti-apartheid movements at the time. I did become wary of some of those who expressed their anti-racism so vehemently when I discovered that they hadn't made a single relationship with a coloured or black person. I began to realise that we can sometimes protest most strongly against things that we have not faced up to within ourselves. This proved useful in later work with sectarianism in Northern Ireland when we had to help one another acknowledge our gut feelings as part of the process of transcending them.

Where there were sufficient numbers of students from a given nationality they often formed a National Students Association such as the Nigerian Students' Association or the Pakistan Students' Association. It was shortly after I began this ministry that the very serious civil war broke out in Nigeria as the province of Biafra sought independence. This had immediate and drastic implications for many of the students, especially those from Biafra. The Student Association split and each day I was assailed with stories of conflict and suffering. Even Church of Scotland missionaries found themselves involved on both sides of the war.

At the pastoral level this had severe repercussions for students from Biafra whose parents and friends were most directly exposed to the effects of the war. Many of them were accompanied by their wives and young families and the loss of fraternal relations with other Nigerian students was very painful indeed. How often I listened to the stories and explanations from each side, each in its own way so logical and understandable but often mutually contradictory. It wasn't long before I was to hear the same stories from Nationalist and Unionist in my own native province. Where does justice lie? How hard it is for us to walk in each other's shoes or to disentangle from many different stories the whole truth.

I remember well reflecting with Pakistani students whether or not they could ever envisage such a split within their nation. They assured me that the bond of Moslem brotherhood was so strong that such an event was inconceivable. It wasn't long after that when I began to hear stories from Eastern Pakistani students telling of terrible atrocities being committed in their homeland by the army (which was largely made up of Western Pakistanis). I was puzzled by these stories because nothing appeared in the world news sections of the national newspapers, yet the testimony from the students' letters was so vivid and convincing. It took three months before the world news took this up in a serious way and, when it did, everything that I had been hearing was confirmed. It was not long before a full-scale tragedy was being played out on the world stage with India nearly being drawn into the war. Finally, the new state of Bangaladesh was born out of the ashes of the conflict.

This is not the place to analyse all the complex factors at work in both of these disputes but it was a time of sharp learning for me personally and a challenge to reflect on the nature of human conflict and the difficulties of peacemaking. More immediately, it was a time for standing beside students far from home as they experienced anguish and despair and a sense of helplessness. What words of compassion or hope could I bring to them from my Christian faith? Above all I learned to listen and avoid clichés.

The encounter with other faith traditions was sometimes developed in a more systematic way in co-operation with the Department of Religious Studies at the University and I found it valuable to share in seminars with young philosophers like Keith Ward who later became a prominent Christian theologian. In addition to David Millar, I found myself often working closely with Catholic chaplains Gerry Hughes (Glasgow University) and Columba Ryan (Strathclyde) and in the new atmosphere created by Vatican II this proved to be a good preparation for later ministry in Ireland.

As indicated, a significant part of the work was the pastoral care of wives and families and this was largely undertaken by a deaconess, Catherine McLintock. Due to cultural patterns it would have been unacceptable for me to visit some of the women in the absence of their husbands, so Catherine's work was invaluable and helped many of them to escape from isolation and loneliness. We were also drawn into developments in the city at large to improve communication between different ethnic minorities and improve race relations.

I was forced to reflect on the whole subject of Christian mission in an increasingly pluralistic society as I met and encountered people from such diverse backgrounds and beliefs. In what ways had the spread of Christianity been associated too closely with Western imperialism? Were we now beginning to experience a backlash? Could we learn to share our Christian convictions from a position of humility and weakness instead of triumphalism? What could we learn from other faiths? How can Christian faith contribute to peacemaking? Why does Christianity and other faiths often aggravate conflict? Questions, Questions, Questions.

As I pondered these questions I was only too aware that the situation in Northern Ireland was worsening by the day. We had kept up our contacts with Corrymeela by returning for several weeks each summer and helping out at family weeks and workcamps. However, I had a growing feeling that I needed to return to Ireland and be in closer solidarity with those who were trying to keep a vision of reconciliation alive in the face of near civil war. I was asked to consider two options, one a congregation in North Antrim near to the Corrymeela Centre and the other a student chaplaincy based in Dublin. After much wrestling and searching for guidance we decided to go to Dublin. Perhaps it was time for me to try to understand the majority culture of the island from its heartland. Before doing so we made a family trip to Europe, including a visit to the Taizé Community in France that left a deep impression on us all, especially through its worship.

CHAPTER 5

THE OTHER IRELAND

ENCOUNTER WITH THE SOUTH

'The term 'ecumenical movement' indicates the initiatives and activities encouraged and organised, according to the various needs of the Church and as opportunities offer, to promote Christian Unity. These are: first, every effort to avoid expressions, judgements and actions which do not represent the condition of our separated brethren with truth and fairness and so make mutual relationships with them more difficult ...
Finally, all are led to examine their own faithfulness to Christ's will for the Church and, wherever necessary, undertake with vigour the task of renewal and reform'

From the *Decree on Ecumenism*
Vatican II

I wasn't a complete stranger to Dublin. My father had many connections there due to his interest in horses and my uncle and cousins had lived there for a period. Also, Shirley and I had spent our honeymoon there in January 1960. However, it was a very changing Dublin that we encountered in 1971. The first full impact of Vatican II was beginning to make itself felt, especially amongst the religious orders. The 'virus' of secularism was beginning to permeate conservative Catholic society. Contraceptives were becoming widely available contrary to the teaching of *Humanae Vitae*. Feminism was emerging to challenge a very male dominated culture. But the forces of conservative resistance were also alive and well.

The attitudes to the Northern conflict were very ambivalent. The Haughey-Blaney arms trial had led to a degree of panic by Jack Lynch (Taoiseach). There was a deep-seated fear that the conflict might spread to the South and destroy the cosy political consensus that had emerged after such a painful history following on the earlier civil war. Those from the older republican tradition were becoming more and more strident and the split in the movement between Provisionals and Officials was causing serious tensions. The vast majority wanted to close their eyes and hope that the North would float off in the direction of Iceland. However, a small minority of people was beginning to seek a responsible way of engaging with the issues without oversimplifying them.

After some househunting we ended up living in North Dublin close to Ballymun because the housing allowance, £8,000, permitted us to have more space there for our four children (Neil, our fourth, had been born in Glasgow). We were in the midst of a predominantly Catholic community, very different from Dublin 4 (with its old Anglo-Irish Protestant tradition). It provided a more realistic opportunity to meet grassroots Dublin Catholics.

My responsibilities were mainly in Trinity College but I also had the pastoral care of the small numbers of Presbyterian students at UCD and at several other smaller Dublin colleges that brought me into contact with a wide cross-section of Dublin society. The impact of the Troubles in the North were illustrated in one way by the fact that the number of Presbyterian students at Trinity College fell from 400 to well under 100 during the four and a half years of my time there. This was almost completely due to the fall in the number of Northern Protestant students and was part of the growing alienation between North and South of the island in the early 70s.

Trinity itself was undergoing a significant period of change, moving from what had been a predominantly Protestant institution to one that was more representative of Irish society as a whole. My arrival coincided with the first official appointment of a Catholic chaplain, Father Brendan Heffernan, and the shared use of Trinity College chapel was probably an ecumenical first in Ireland. A small minority of Catholics had been attending Trinity College for many years but they did so without the permission of the Archbishop John

Charles McQuaid. But now that the ban had been lifted the number of Catholic students began to rise rapidly.

The warmth and support of my predecessor, Brian McConnell and his wife Molly, together with the help of Billy and Joyce Moran from Abbey Presbyterian church, made the welcome for our family very positive. Indeed, the influence of the congregation at Abbey was very significant in the lives of us all. It was a matter of great sadness to us when Billy's health suddenly deteriorated and he died shortly after Christmas 1973. However, before that I became aware of his pioneering ecumenical ministry in co-operation with the Church of Ireland and Catholic Church in the Gardiner Street area and the social outreach to disadvantaged families in the district. Alan Martin, his successor, carried on and developed this tradition in important ways.

Because of the strong links which some of the Northern students had with Corrymeela, notably Liz Maxwell (later Parkin), we were able to form an interdenominational group to maintain our interest and support for the work of reconciliation and peacemaking. Those issues suddenly became focused in a way that I will not easily forget. Barely five months after my arrival the events of Bloody Sunday took place in Derry on 30 January 1972. The impact in Dublin was dramatic. A day of mourning was proclaimed and the intensity of anti-British feeling which filled the air was potent with danger. Still driving a British registered car we often felt quite vulnerable to random attacks. The climax came with the burning down of the British Embassy in Merrion Square.

Because of my links with UCD, I was invited to take part in a special ceremony for students on the actual Day of Mourning and to make a small contribution. The chairperson for this event was Professor Dudley Edwards (the Professor of History). Dennis Cooke (Methodist Chaplain) and myself asked for a meeting prior to the event in order to clarify the whole basis of the meeting. We were afraid that we were going to be railroaded into an openly anti-British event that would leave no space for acknowledging the shared responsibility of all of us for such a tragedy. Thankfully we were able to establish sufficient common ground to go ahead, but it was a very painful time for us all.

The over-reaction of this period gave way to a more measured reflection and growing concern lest the whole island be thrown into conflict. The positive effects of Vatican II were expressed in many invitations to speak and share my tradition, especially by the Religious Orders. The Jesuits, Redemptorists, Holy Ghost Fathers, The Divine Word Missionaries and the Columbans were amongst those with whom I found warm and enriching relationships. It was during this time that the Irish School of Ecumenics was founded by Father Michael Hurley, SJ. The charismatic renewal movement in Ireland was also born and crossed all the old divides, although it sometimes allowed its enthusiasm to become manipulative. The rediscovery of the Scriptures by ordinary Catholics was bringing a fresh burst of life to many.

On the peace front there were a number of movements emerging who wished to contribute to reconciliation and several of them came together to form the Glencree Centre for Reconciliation. Because of my Corrymeela connections I became involved here as a bridge person. The driving force in this movement were people like Una O'Higgins O'Malley (the daughter of Kevin O'Higgins, the first Minister of Justice in the Free State Government and who was murdered by the IRA in 1927), Frank Purcell (an Australian priest on the leadership team of the Columban Missionary Order), Shaun Curran, (a local priest), Rachel Bewley (from a famous Irish Quaker family), Ivor O'Sullivan (a Chemistry lecturer in UCD) and Geoffrey Corry (an active Methodist youth leader). The focus for the development of the project was the rehabilitation of an old reform school, which had once been a British Army barracks for putting down the rebels of the 1798 Rising! This was located in the Wicklow mountains a few miles out of South Dublin, in a very beautiful setting.

This is not the place for a history of Glencree but a few comments are in order. Because the original group contained many very strong individuals it was not easy to weld them into a cohesive group. Corrymeela has been fortunate in that our original leader, Ray Davey, was a unifying factor in himself and there were no serious competitors for the position. In addition, his deep and profound experiences as a YMCA worker and prisoner of war during World War II gave him certain qualities that proved to be invaluable. He was, above all, an 'enabler', always looking for ways to unlock the gifts of others and help them to find their place. In that sense he was a 'community maker'.

However, in spite of difficulties and tensions, Glencree has made a significant contribution to the work of reconciliation in Ireland and has been a focus for work on that essential North-South dimension of the task. It has become more and more clear to me over the years that unless the north-south and east-west dimensions of the Northern Ireland problem are tackled as well as the internal work in the North, then the wounds of our history cannot be healed. The words of Charles Haughey (himself a very ambivalent politician) concerning the 'totality of relationships' have come to be recognised as the essential foundation for any peace process. It was therefore from this time in 1972 that some of us came to the conclusion that an essential dimension of the work for peace must involve the creation of a new relationship between the British and Irish governments and peoples.

After Bloody Sunday these relationships appeared to be at an all time low so the task of building them seemed awesome to put it mildly. However, at this time I began to recognise a number of people of influence who were questioning the simplistic attitudes of the past and were beginning to create a new consciousness. Notable amongst these were Garret Fitzgerald and Conor Cruise O'Brien. In addition to reflective articles and other contributions they began to appear publicly in protest against the IRA campaign of violence, which was now escalating rapidly in the wake of Bloody Sunday. Both of them showed the courage of their convictions by travelling to the North and trying to report as objectively as possible on the facts as they perceived them. Conor's book *States of Ireland* was a kind of landmark in journalistic reflection that exposed the ambivalence of so many actors in the drama that was being played out. His critique of aspects of the Nationalist and Republican tradition has been severe and insightful and deserves to be pondered by all. Unfortunately it has led him in recent years to be too cynical about the motives of Republicans in the peace process and not sufficiently critical of Unionist prejudice. Unfortinately he has allowed himself to be used by those who are not open to change and who refuse to recognise the flaws in the past Stormont regime.

Garret Fitzgerald, who ultimately became Taoiseach, had a natural empathy for both traditions as a result of being the child of a mixed marriage. This led him to a fair-minded assessment of many issues and a willingness to work patiently for changes in Nationalist policy and better relationships with Britain. This empathy was nowhere better illustrated than after he had shared a room at Corrymeela with a Community Relations policeman and subsequently wrote an article for the *Irish Times*. In this article he praised the courage and compassion of the policeman and broke down some of the hard stereotypes that were becoming widespread.

One small initiative that the chaplains in Trinity College took was to launch a series of public lectures on the theme 'Violence and Social Change'. One of the contributors to this series was Conor Cruise O'Brien and the hall was packed to the door for his contribution. His lecture was a searing critique of the basis of the republican campaign of violence and an expression of his conviction that it could only succeed in making things worse. Another contributor to that series on the theme of reconciliation was Ray Davey from Corrymeela who shared some of the moving personal stories of the work of keeping bridges open in the midst of community chaos.

The events of the Sunningdale Agreement and the creation of the Power Sharing Executive were very present in our minds as we hoped and prayed for a new start. Sadly it was not to be, as the Ulster Workers Strike swept away the fragile plant before it had time to build confidence and consensus. The problems of Ted Heath's government due to the miners' strike, followed by the general election, when a Labour government was elected, destroyed the continuity of ministerial responsibility for Northern Ireland and gravely weakened the position of the new executive. The general election provided the anti-Sunningdale forces in Unionism with the chance to exploit the fears of the grass roots and to claim that there was no mandate for the experiment. The legacy of 1974 was a massive increase in paramilitary loyalist groups like the UDA and the UVF and the inevitable increase in sectarian killings.

Dublin itself was to be a target of one of these attacks and on one day the worst fatality record of all the troubles took place in Dublin and Monaghan. The fears of the spread of the troubles now seemed to be justified. Since our return from Scotland to Ireland our contacts with the ongoing work of Corrymeela were now much more regular as we travelled up to Community meetings and other activities. However, disruption of rail services was a regular feature of the time and I well remember one occasion when we moved from train to bus at Dundalk, back to the train at Portadown, only to be told that the line was blocked again. At this point the weary travellers headed for the Ulsterbus depot only to be told there was a bus strike. However, we noticed the bus returning to Dundalk moving out of the car park and we managed to persuade the driver to take us to Belfast, in spite of his fear of pickets.

During my period in Dublin, I began a study of the whole theme of reconciliation and peacemaking, with special reference to the role of the churches in Ireland and this was later to be presented to the Theological Faculty of QUB for a PhD. The more I reflected on this theme the more it became apparent to me that the ministry of reconciliation was far from central in the life and work of Irish churches, Catholic and Protestant. Our history of conflict over the generations had left us in the position of being chaplains to two divided communities. To move out of this stance into a ministry of the whole of society was a painful journey that threatened the identity of many church members. The ecumenical movement had such big implications for a divided island and a divided society that it was perceived as 'a sell-out' or betrayal both politically and ecclessialogically by many, especially from the Protestant community.

And yet the imperative was clear for anyone reading the Gospel accounts. As Ray Davey put it so succinctly, 'Unless the churches can speak a word of reconciliation we have nothing to say.' I remember speaking to a Mennonite from the USA who had been visiting a school in Ballymena around about this time. She said that none of the pupils could see any connection between the gospel and 'peace'. It was about 'salvation' and in their understanding of 'salvation', 'peace' did not figure at all. My first meeting with a leading Mennonite was when John Howard Yoder visited Trinity College and when I read his book *The Politics of Jesus* it brought the passion story to life in a way which I had not experienced before. The contribution of this Anabaptist tradition, kept alive by the Mennonites, was to prove a significant one in the days ahead. Now that the whole concept of Christendom was disintegrating in the face of an aggressively secular culture, its relevance for all the main line denominations was becoming clear. I will return to this theme later.

In the autumn of 1975 the post of Chaplaincy at Queen's University became vacant and I was offered the chance to move to Belfast. As I was now becoming more heavily involved with the work of Corrymeela again, and in view of the desire to engage more directly with the work of reconciliation within Northern Ireland, it seemed to be an appropriate opportunity. In addition, it was becoming only too obvious that the fall in the number of Presbyterian students in Dublin would soon render my post a part-time one and I would be obliged to combine it with a congregational ministry if I remained much longer. The fact that the conflict in the North was still very intense was obviously a worry for the family, but we felt it was where God wanted us to be, so at Christmas 1975 we moved into the Presbyterian Community Centre flat at 7 College Park East.

CHAPTER 6

RETURN TO THE NORTH

FRACTURED SOCIETY

'In situations of conflict Christians often find themselves accomplices in war, rather than agents of peace. We find it difficult to distance ourselves from ourselves and our own culture and so we echo its reigning opinions and mimic its practices. As we keep the vision of God's future alive, we need to reach across the firing lines and join hands with our brothers and sisters on the other side. We need to let them pull us out of the enclosure of our own culture and its own peculiar set of prejudices so that we can read afresh the 'One Word of God'. In this way we might become once again the salt to the world ridden by strife.'

Miroslav Volf
Exclusion and Embrace
(Abingdon Press 1996)

Although I had been familiar with the state of the city as a result of many visits during our time in Dublin, I don't think the full scale of the destruction hit me until I was a full-time resident again. To wander down McClure Street nearby and see a street where every single house was burnt out, and to be aware that acres of the city were in a similar state, was breathtaking. However, we settled in after Christmas and managed to place our children in Methodist College and the local Botanic Primary School without too much difficulty.

My responsibilities, in addition to being chaplain to 1,500 plus Presbyterian students, was to look after a Centre where there was a small core group of residential students, and provide a social and religious programme for all-comers. Queen's had been a hive of political consciousness in the late 60s and early 70s due to the Civil Rights Movement and many of the students of that period had played a leading role in the movement and some had been involved in Corrymeela. However, after the onset of violence a wholly new situation had emerged. It was much too dangerous to be active in that way now, so the reaction amongst most students was to be preoccupied only with their academic and future career prospects. In addition, as a result of the UCCA Scheme that offered students the possibility of studying in universities in England, Scotland and Wales, sometimes with full grants, there was a growing tendency for the brighter Protestant students to take advantage of this opportunity to get out of Northern Ireland, at least for a spell. Who could blame them? My own family later followed suit. In many cases the long-term outcome was that they did not return to Northern Ireland but found employment in Britain.

The result of all this was that the earlier pattern of social life at the University that I had experienced and that had been nurtured so successfully by Ray and Kathleen Davey, was hard to sustain. In addition, many of the students who lived in Halls or flats returned to their home towns or country areas at the weekends and this was furthered by the increase in student cars. The massive energy that had been such a resource to the Corrymeela Community in the 60s was no longer there.

Nevertheless there was a task to be done and the Centre had some unique facilities that proved to be a major resource not only to students but to a wide variety of groups who were searching for a 'neutral' meeting place during the years 1976-80. Indeed, some of my family found this facility on their doorstep too good to be true. My son Philip, in particular, learnt how to operate the film projector, play the roof chapel organ and arrange practices for his school band in the hall. It reached the point where I had to ask him at times whether I could get a 'booking' myself.

In addition to the ordinary student activities, such as Community meals and snacks, worship, study groups and barn dances, the Centre was let to groups such as returned VSO (Voluntary Service Overseas), The Irish Association and a local youth club, which some students wished to help with as part of their social service to the community. The 'All Children Together' groups also had many of their meetings there as they developed their plans for integrated education, which was to have its first concrete project in the launching of Lagan College. Perhaps the group to which we extended the most hospitality was the new movement called 'The Peace People' which had emerged as a result of a violent incident in the summer of 1977.

The details of this movement are available elsewhere, but a few comments are relevant to the main themes of this memoir. The Belfast Centre of the Corrymeela Community at 8 Upper Crescent (Corrymeela House) had made the attic of their building available to the core organisers of this movement on a temporary basis. The movement developed in the form of rallies and marches, first in Belfast and later in the various towns of the province. Local support groups were set up in various districts to recruit people for the rallies and to consider ways of making a 'peace' witness in their local communities. The leaders felt the need to bring together representatives of the various groups in order to debate policy and direction. It was for this purpose that I was approached to let the Centre to the movement on many occasions.

My wife Shirley became involved in a local Peace People group and many Corrymeela members, including myself and my family, supported the marches. One member of the Corrymeela Community, Peter McLachlan, an activist in the voluntary social work scene, was very close to the leaders and at a later stage became the elected leader. I served on a Special Committee with Peter that allocated money from international sources to grass roots projects for community development, employment creation and community relations.

Some of our experiences on the marches were moving, especially the walk on the Shankill Road, whilst others were scary to put it mildly. The Falls Road march was partially disrupted by IRA supporters and I had to protect my family from wild stone throwing by use of an umbrella as a shield. Thankfully the army did not intervene, otherwise we might have had a blood-bath like Bloody Sunday. I have always had a great respect for the courage of Betty Williams and Mairead Corrigan (Maguire) in this initiative and I think that many people who were apathetic about peacemaking took their first steps as a result of the movement.

However, it was not long before difficulties began to arise. How was the movement to be sustained? Was there a common understanding of what was meant by peace? Did it mean simply the stopping of violence? The leadership group of the two women founders and Ciaran McKeown, a local journalist who had become their close confidant and adviser, developed a Gandhian-type statement based on a totally non-violent philosophy with implications not only for paramilitary groups but also for the emergency powers being operated by the courts, army and police. There was no real opportunity for the mass movement to absorb this philosophy and adopt it democratically. It was simply proclaimed. As the implications of this philosophy began to be expressed by way of public comment on controversial issues, the 'foot soldiers' of the movement began to be wary. They were expected to defend the pronouncements of their leaders and deal with the questions of their neighbours who had read or heard the statements on the media.

Most of the ordinary supporters of the movement were simply at the beginning of a big journey to understand what might be involved in building real foundations for peace. They wanted the violence to end but they were far from united on what was needed to replace it. Some were happy to concentrate on building some cross-community alliances and then tackling some of the local issues and needs in their district that seemed to be relevant to community relationships. A few of these disaffiliated from the main body and concentrated on their local situations. Many others became apathetic when they realised that marching alone in protest was not going to solve our problems.

The award of the Nobel Peace Prize to the leaders did not prove to be a blessing. It led to controversy about the use of the prize-money and to a dangerous tendency to become commentators on international issues all over the world. Many of those who had carried the burden of the day and were closely associated with the leaders felt excluded from the inner circle and from having a real say on policy. Nevertheless, as I have already said, many people did take their first step in peace making and helped to create a variety of local initiatives tackling issues such as the support of the bereaved, work with youth at risk, civil liberties action and inter-church reconciliation.

During our period at the Presbyterian Community Centre, our family faced some times of stress and difficulty. My wife Shirley's father died suddenly and she had to travel to Edinburgh to make the funeral arrangements with her brother. Unfortunately she had just had a serious domestic accident, when a pressure cooker had exploded leaving her with serious burns on her arms and body. Her mother had died suddenly in the early 60s when we were at Kilmakee, so she was now without both of her parents. Her father had married again but his second wife was not in good mental or physical health. I was unable to attend the funeral because someone had to stay with the children in Belfast and it was not a practical possibility for all of us to go.

On another occasion, on a Sunday evening, the IRA attempted to bomb the Computer Centre that was situated just opposite our front door. We were in the middle of our meal, so we all fled to the other end of the building. My daughter, Alison, immediately grabbed the cat, to which she was devoted, thus illustrating her priorities 'in a moment of crisis'! Fortunately the damage was slight, apart from a few windows. However, there were several fatal incidents close to us during that period, sometimes as a result of booby traps and some others were seriously injured. The News each evening brought further examples of atrocities in all parts of the province.

Another issue that occupied much of my attention during this period was the struggle within the Presbyterian Church in Ireland in relation to our membership of the World Council of Churches (WCC). The involvement of the WCC in the struggles against racism and the work of decolonisation produced a crisis of confidence within our church. The 'Programme to Combat Racism' that had given grants to Black Liberation movements in Southern Africa, albeit for social and humanitarian needs, produced a wave of protest. The WCC was accused of supporting violence and their actions were compared with that of supporting the IRA. In addition to that, the rise of sectarianism in our troubles had produced a resistance to the new movement of dialogue with the Roman Catholic Church that had emerged as a result of Vatican II.

Although many of us were aware that the WCC should not be immune from criticism, we felt that the only way to contribute constructively was by remaining in membership. The ecumenical movement was a journey that we were called to stay on, in obedience to the teaching of Jesus, and a move towards withdrawal would cut us off from our brothers and sisters in Christ. Attempting to put the case for our continued membership led to an intense struggle in which vitriolic propaganda against the WCC was fed into our already fear-ridden community.

Sadly we were defeated in this struggle and a deep sense of depression settled upon many of us as we saw our church take yet another step away from the centrality of the ministry of reconciliation. During this period and following it, many ministers found it almost impossible to sustain a peace-making ministry. Many quietly sought other charges in Scotland or England and in a few cases they were forced to resign. One lesson I did learn from this experience was how easy it is to allow such a struggle to corrupt one's own attitudes. When subjected to hate, distrust and scorn, it is so easy to allow similar attitudes to take root in oneself. The call to love our enemies is never more difficult than in relation to opponents within one's own family or tribe. Without deeper spiritual resources we would not be able to sustain the attitudes necessary for a ministry of reconciliation.

All of this only emphasised the continuing importance of Corrymeela as some kind of countersign in our broken society and a source of support for those who were in danger of submitting to despair. 'It is better to light a candle than curse the darkness,' or in the Irish version, 'It's better to light ten candles even if nine blow out!' I was now very actively involved in the life and work of the Corrymeela Community, a member of the Council and of the programme planning group. Our awareness of the need to provide alternatives for young people who were in danger of being drawn into paramilitary groups had led to the appointment of Derick Wilson as Centre Director and Billy Kane as a full-time youth worker. Both of these had been engaged at the coalface of youth work and Derick had also been in youth training, so they were equipped with the contacts and some of the skills for the challenge. Harold Good, our Centre Director since 1973 had, together with Ray Davey, overseen a major development of the Centre and its buildings, so that a new thrust in this work was now more feasible.

Our work with victims was given a special focus as a result of an initiative by Maura Kiely. Maura and Edmond Kiely had recently suffered the loss of their son, Gerard, in a sectarian shooting as he left St Brigid's Church after attending Mass. After a period of grief and anger, Maura decided on the advice of a priest friend to visit other bereaved people and to invite them to meet together. The priest in question was Jim McEvoy, Professor of Scholastic Philosophy at Queen's and a friend of Ray Davey and myself. He asked Ray if the group could meet at Corrymeela House, the Belfast Centre of the Corrymeela Community. The group, entitled The Cross Group, has continued to support bereaved families for over twenty years now and has often made use of our Centre at Ballycastle as well as our Belfast house.

Jim McEvoy was also supportive of another initiative associated with Corrymeela, the Northern Ireland Mixed Marriage Association. As anyone who knows the province of Northern Ireland knows, those who crossed our religious/cultural divide by daring to fall in love and get married can often be made to feel that they are betraying the cause in either church or politics or both. As a result of a conference at our Centre earlier in the 70s, a group of such couples decided to set up a support group and to offer a counselling service to prospective couples. Jim found himself involved for the very practical reason that his brother Paddy had married a Presbyterian girl (Hazel). Over the years this group has shared their experience with the churches and have managed to influence them in the direction of a much more humane and pastoral approach, in spite of remaining unresolved theological difficulties.

Over this period the continued stress on Ray Davey's health and the fact that he was nearing retiring age was raising the question of a possible successor. After a period of exploration of possible candidates, I was elected to become the next Leader of the Community. To follow in Ray and Kathleen's footsteps would indeed be an arduous task, but Shirley and I both had a deep sense that this was what we were called to do. My many experiences in Parish ministry, with overseas students and in other chaplaincies, including my spell in Dublin, all seemed to have been a preparation for this. My work on researching the whole concept of reconciliation and peacemaking was to prove an important resource for the days ahead, when any reading had to be fitted into a hectic timetable.

It was a time of considerable family change too. My father had died just after Christmas after a period of gradual failing health. We had expected this to bring some relief to my mother who had cared for him to the point of exhaustion for a long period. We were later to realise that the vacuum that this left was so great that she would find it impossible to cope with the loneliness. Sadly, it was not long until she was affected by Alzheimer's Disease that ultimately led to her spending the last three and a half years of her life in a Nursing Home. I have to confess that the greatest part of the burden of these years was carried by my brother and sister, for which I am eternally grateful.

As we prepared to wind up our duties at the Presbyterian Centre and to find a place for the family to live, our eldest son, Duncan, was about to depart for Oxford University. Our income was such that he was able to obtain the maximum grant, otherwise it would have been quite impossible. Indeed, without a temporary loan from the Corrymeela Community we would not have been able to get any Building Society to give us a mortgage. Eventually we obtained a house in College Park Avenue, no more than a couple of hundred yards down the road from the Presbyterian Community Centre. Apart from the piano we moved all our furniture by wheelbarrow! As I realised I would be commuting a lot to Ballycastle, it was good to have a house close to my new Belfast base in Upper Crescent and thus avoid double commuting.

CHAPTER 7

CORRYMEELA AND THE MINISTRY OF PEACEMAKING

'But now in union with Christ Jesus you who once were far off have been brought near through the shedding of Christ's blood. For he himself is our peace. Gentiles and Jews he has made the two one; and in his own body of flesh and blood has broken down the enmity which stood as a dividing wall between them; for he annulled the law with its rules and regulations so as to create out of the two a single new humanity in himself, thereby making peace. This was his purpose, to reconcile the two in a single body to God through the cross, on which he killed the enmity.'

Ephesians 2: 13-16
(New English Bible 1961)

On my appointment to the leadership of the Community the Council had asked Derick Wilson (Centre Director) and myself to agree to visit a number of Dutch Christian Adult Education Centres and to meet some people in frontier ministries in Holland. This was in response to an offer to the Community by the Dutch Northern Irish Committee, whose Secretary, David Stevens, was the chairperson of the Corrymeela Council (and Associate Secretary of the Irish Council of Churches – later full Secretary).

This wasn't my first contact with this group, which had emerged as a result of a request made to the European churches for help in training for Northern Ireland. A Joint Committee had been set up with equal membership from Northern Ireland and Holland on an inter-church basis. At first they had invited many groups to Holland, partly to reflect on their home situations from a distance and also to meet with appropriate groups in the Netherlands. In addition to church groups, this often included police and grass roots community groups. Among other things, the Dutch offered their skills in facilitating honest conversation and reflection on some of the thorny issues of our divided society. However, the cost of bringing groups to Holland led them to look for ways and places of working within Northern Ireland and they wished to explore the possibilities of greater cooperation with Corrymeela.

Our visit took place in early January during an intensely cold period and I won't easily forget the experience of standing at tram stops or railway stations on cold frosty mornings as we made our way to the various appointments that had been made for us. Our chief organiser was Rev Aat van Rhijn whom I had met along with another member of the team, Fr Andre Lascaris, a Dominican theologian, on a previous visit. It was a very useful experience that enabled Derick and myself to strengthen our relationship and to prepare for a close partnership in the life and work of the Community. During our visit we made the acquaintance of another member of the team, Roel Kaptein, and our later partnership with him was to be a significant stage in the Corrymeela journey for many of us (of that more later).

Derick Wilson had already initiated some important policy changes in the shape of the one-year volunteer team and in the development of our work with 'youth at risk' in our turbulent society. The new 'Serve and Learn' programme for the volunteers had a built-in focus on reconciliation as a result of selecting young people from many different social, religious and national backgrounds. It was geared to help young people deal with difference and to learn how to build community on the basis of mutual acceptance. This is always a painful as well as joyful process. It forced all of us, staff, members and volunteers to reflect deeply on the resources of our faith, if we were not to destroy each other in the process.

We received help from many sources in this learning about life in community and in particular from Jean Vanier, the founder of the L'Arche communities. Having faced up to the experience of living together with mentally handicapped adults, Jean had realised some of the most profound truths about Christian community that applied widely to all. His classic model spoke of three phases:

Phase 1 This is the romantic phase when our new found delight in sharing with others runs the danger of idealising one another. Everyone is an Angel. **Phase 2** comes when we realise that the others are not the saints we thought they were and we become disillusioned. Instead of being angels some of our fellow members are becoming devils.
Phase 3 comes when we have learnt something about acceptance and forgiveness and when our own self-knowledge has enabled us to understand how we are accepted in God's love and so can accept one another. As Dietrich Bonhoeffer once said, it is much easier to love our 'dream of a Christian community' than the actual people God has given us to live with.

The appointment of Billy Kane as Youth Worker and Rosie Walsh as Volunteer Co-ordinator led to the development of a very creative approach to work with young adults, which was later to be named as 'Seed Groups'. The essence of this approach was to nurture a process of sharing stories, listening and reflection on the many different aspects of their life experience. To begin with, the themes were related to family, peer group, sexuality, etc., where those from differing religious, social or political backgrounds had plenty of common ground. Later on in the six-weekend programme they shared their experiences of religious, cultural and political formation. Having now established fairly strong relationships, it was possible to listen to each other through this much more difficult territory and to move towards that deeper acceptance which becomes possible. Over the years these programmes have been developed and modified for use by a wide variety of groups, including school groups, youth and adults from many different backgrounds. Another member of staff who contributed much to this process was the Rev Doug Baker who had been appointed as a result of a very generous offer by the Presbyterian Church of the USA. A further appointment of Fr Gerry Cassidy, a Redemptrist priest, was of special significance because it became possible for many of the young people to meet and get to know a Catholic priest as a real human being, perhaps for the first time. The invitations that Gerry later received to visit youth fellowships in Protestant churches are amongst the most moving aspects of his experience of ministry. He was trusted!

Meantime we were beginning to get to know Roel Kaptein from Holland as he led us in a number of sessions for staff and community training. The first experience of this was far from painless for many of us. This was partly the result of a culture clash as we experienced his approach to be so direct and abrasive that some of us were in danger of 'retiring hurt' and licking our wounds. However, as Roel himself mellowed and adapted a little to our Irish ways, some of us began to learn some important new insights about human relations and the dynamics of conflict. We began to understand and acknowledge the degree of manipulation that was often occurring in our relationships and the subtle ways in which we could often scapegoat each other.

Although some of this work remains controversial within the Community, and amongst wider groups involved in reconciliation, it has had a profound influence upon many members and staff and has touched on our work with churches, families, youth, community work, psychiatry and politics. Only a very brief reference to this is possible here but something needs to be said in order to provide an introduction for those who might like to go into it more fully.

Perhaps the key insight develops from an understanding of human behaviour and learning as largely based on 'mimesis'. This is much more than 'imitation' since it operates largely at an unconscious level. However, in human society this mimesis is based not merely on the behaviour of the other model but on the *desires* of the model, i.e. it is a 'mimesis of desire'. This desire could be a material object but it could also be something like 'status' or in its most subtle form 'metaphysical desire'. It operates on the principle that I desire an object *not for itself* but because *the other* desires it. Indeed if the other ceases to desire the object it is no longer desirable for me.

Once caught up in this kind of mimesis there is an inherent tendency to move towards rivalry, conflict and ultimately to *violence*, unless there is some restraining factor. All societies are aware of the danger of this kind of conflict and try to prevent it by various prohibitions. The most subtle form of dealing with it is the *scapegoat mechanism*. In order to avoid the chaos of many conflicts a group seizes on one group or individual and marks them out as the cause of the conflict. The person or group may be chosen for some random difference of appearance or other distinguishing characteristic, but usually they are no more guilty than others. However, they act as a unifying force for the rest of the society as they seek to expel them. The mechanism is unconscious and although it is based on a 'lie', the fact that it produces a kind of peace convinces everyone of its apparent 'truth'.

René Girard, who developed this insight, regards the history of the Jewish Community as the one exception where the lie inherent in the scapegoat mechanism began to be exposed. The God of Israel, in contrast to the Gods of other societies, was perceived not as the God of the scapegoaters. Instead, their God was identified with the scapegoats. When they are downtrodden in Egypt and expelled, they are assured that their God identified with them. Of course, the people of Israel do not fully grasp this and from time to time forget that they are called to expose all scapegoaters. They get into mimesis with the powerful nations and scapegoat their own poor, but the prophets expose them and recall them to their vocation.

The climax of the whole story is in the life and death of Jesus. In this final drama the nature of the scapegoat mechanism is fully exposed. The attempt to make a scapegoat out of Jesus fails because he unmasks the deception that is involved and those who were close to him know that he is innocent of the charges brought against him. At the same time he freely takes upon himself our violence and offers us forgiveness. For those who recognise the meaning of this event, a new beginning is possible. It is now possible to build community without scapegoating others as we are set free from this mimesis of desire through our relationship with Jesus.

The particular aspect of Jesus' relationship to the Father is one in which he is free from the mimesis of desire. He is not in rivalry with the Father (Philippians 2). He seeks the Father's will and obeys it. In mimesis with him, we can be set free from the mimesis of desire and enter into that same freedom of knowing and doing God's will. Of course, this is a life long process and, living as we do in a world of rivalry and violence and desire, we are often caught up in that. But as our relationship with Christ deepens we can more and more enter into that freedom. Ultimately it is the freedom to love in the sense of seeking the good of the other out of the knowledge and experience that we are loved.

The insights that can be developed here help us to recognise the ways in which we tend to become involved in scapegoating or in colluding with it in our daily life. We have begun to see the significance of this is our community life, in our churches and in the wider politics of society. Many of our members have used it in community relations work, in mediation and in understanding conflict. Some of the pamphlets developed by the Faith and Politics group (an initiative of Corrymeela, Glencree and the Irish School of Ecumenics) have used these insights to illuminate the challenges of relating to ex-prisoners, bereaved victims and various aspects of the peace process.

As Leader of the Community my responsibility was not only to support and guide the work of our Centres but also to encourage the ordinary members in their own local situations or special callings. Over the years the Community was to become more and more diverse, changing from the very student centred group of the 60s to one that included people from every walk of life. Our work with families under stress had thrown us into contact with people who were giving leadership at the heart of grass roots communities and some of these, like Margaret and Gerry Mulvenna, had become full members. A number of couples from inter-church marriages had also found Corrymeela geared to their needs as well as offering them a chance to share the richness of their experience of life. The tragedies of bereavement had linked us with many of those who had suffered deeply and those, like Maura and Edmund Kiely, who became full members found support and opportunity to move beyond victimhood and to become key agents in the work of reconciliation through their outreach to others.

One of the tensest periods in the life of the Community was during the hunger strikes of the early eighties. Both the events themselves and the way they were being handled led to wide differences of view within our membership. At the same time there was the need to respond to families caught up in the tension, who needed to get away for periods of stress relief. We learnt a lot about the limits of rational debate in a situation where our gut reactions were very different – depending on our cultural and religious background. We had to learn, in sometimes painful ways, to hear each other, without trying to convince each other that 'we were right'. We learnt that part of reconciliation involves living and accepting unresolved issues at times, as well as honesty and openness. As I mentioned earlier, one of the sources of spiritual guidance which we drew on during difficult periods, when the wider conflicts were very intense, were occasional visits to our Centre of Jean Vanier, founder of the L'Arche Communities. Those Communities of mentally handicapped living together with others had opened up new insights into life in community that were applicable to us all. The encounter with those who are vulnerable, yet open and honest, can enable us to acknowledge our own vulnerability, remove our masks and rediscover our humanity. In a profound sense we can meet Jesus there. (I have written about this in more detail in my book *Journey of Hope*.) We continue to learn from the L'Arche Communities and many of our members and volunteers have spent periods of time sharing in them in different parts of the world.

Michael Earle replaced Derick Wilson as Centre Director in 1985. He and his wife Anne had been involved earlier in the student work groups organised by Ray Davey. They had eventually moved to live and work in New Zealand, so it was a very big jump to return to such an onerous task in the midst of a very divided society. Following Derick Wilson was not an easy path to walk in and the contrast in style of leadership and management was a difficult adjustment for all concerned. It was another painful process of learning on the road of reconciliation that revealed to us all some of our deep-seated prejudices. Although educated at QUB, Mike was from an English public school background and the clash with some of the Ulster cultural styles of working was often difficult for all parties. I found myself caught in the difficult position of hearing the real pain of the staff who were not at ease with Mike's style of working and at the same time needing to challenge what I felt to be some anti-Brit prejudice at work here. It was also clear that this prejudice was coming not only from those with a Catholic/nationalist background! This was another reminder of the complex relationships between all of us in these islands which is part of the agenda of reconciliation. Some of us learnt to recognise this a bit more honestly as time went on and to realise afresh that all relationships are a two-way street. I have the greatest respect for Mike's willingness to work at this process of communication and ultimately to win deep respect for his integrity and sincerity and recognition of some of his outstanding gifts. It was with real sadness that we bade Mike, Anne and family farewell when they moved back to New Zealand after a five-year stint.

With the rise of Sinn Féin as a significant political force in the wake of the hunger strikes, some of us became involved in attempts to create dialogue with them and also to promote wider meetings between elected politicians to see if the stalemate that had arisen could be broken. Louis Boyle, who was Chairperson of Council at the time, played an important part in this process. Sinn Féin was particularly keen to meet with people from a Protestant background in order to understand something more of their sense of identity and their resistance (in the main) to a United Ireland. I think they were beginning to recognise that attempts to force a million people to give up their Britishness would not work and that they would have to make some compromises if any political settlement was to be possible. The meetings were important in that they helped all of us to recognise each other's humanity and to see how much we had in common in spite of our differences. In many ways these meetings and many others helped to create a climate in which the later peace process became possible.

Most of the work of Corrymeela was best carried out 'low key', without any major publicity. This was partly because we did not wish to put any of the groups that we worked with under any pressure from those who were opposed to our work on sectarian grounds. However, we did feel that from time to time we needed to raise our profile in order to awaken interest in the wider church and society and to provide opportunities for others to share in the ministry of reconciliation.

One of the ways in which we did this was through our Summerfest programmes, largely carried through by the organising skill of Doug Baker, but with wide involvement from Community members and friends. The idea emerged from Ray Davey, our founder, as a result of his involvement in the German Kirchentag events. He suggested that we attempt to host a festival on a smaller scale, but one that would present a marketplace of ideas, workshops and fresh approaches to worship and Christian action for reconciliation in Ireland and the wider world. The events were open to all ages, making it possible for parents and children to participate fully and they had a strong international as well as an Irish dimension. Key speakers and leaders from other countries included Mother Teresa (of Calcutta), Jim Wallis (Sojourners Community, Washington DC), Fr Elias Chacour (Israel), Rev Alan Boesak (South Africa), Dr Sheila Cassidy and many others. All of these people were able to bring the experience of working in situations of conflict and suffering and share their insight with us all. More recently Senator George Mitchell was a significant contributor. But at the heart of the event were contributors who were working at the coalface in church and society and a few key leaders such as Dr John Dunlop, Cardinal Daly, Rev Dr Eric Gallagher, Rev Ruth Patterson and (President to be) Mary McAleese.

In addition to providing a wider vehicle for participation, this festival acted as a support for many people struggling to keep the flame of reconciliation alive, often against great odds, in their local situations. It gave those who felt isolated a sense that they were not alone and it challenged others, who were still only putting their 'toe in the water', to take a bigger step forward. As a marketplace of ideas it opened up possibilities for work with all ages and showed where resources and skills were available to give confidence. Above all, it was a time of shared worship and the renewal of vision for all who were coping with times of doubt and despair. The emphasis in all the events was on the 'Coming of the Kingdom' with biblical passages such as the Lord's Prayer, the Beatitudes, the parables of the Kingdom, etc., providing a foundation for all the wide spectrum of events. The lighter side of life was well catered for in clowning, drama and concerts with artists such as Tom Paxton and the Sands Brothers topping the bill. When the weather was fine the scene on our glorious cliff top site was truly magic. However, the Irish weather and the North Atlantic winds kept a note of reality alive and on many days we struggled to keep our marquees upright and to prevent all and sundry being washed away! The efforts of young volunteers and the maintenance staff at our Centre, together with the miraculous work of our catering team, was truly praiseworthy. It was indeed a team effort that tested us all to the full.

The less dramatic but in no sense less important work of our summer programme, and the ongoing programmes of the Centre throughout the whole year with youth and family groups, continued to be the backbone of the work at our Centre. It was the place where relationships were built, where support was given to those under stress, where dialogue of all kinds took place and deep wounds were sometimes healed or at least made easier to bear. This work continued even in the midst of the endless community crises which made all plans subject to uncertainty. And the staff at our Centres, together with the many volunteers (including Community members), made them places of welcome and care for thousands of visitors and guests.

No wonder we were exhausted at times. We did not always care for ourselves and each other in the way that we needed to if we were to be able to receive our guests with openness and sensitivity. We tried to do too much and at times failed to renew our spiritual resources. We had to learn the hard way about what is involved in living in community. By the grace of God and the help of many wise people, we learnt some of the lessons about the meaning of reconciliation; about acceptance and forgiveness; about honesty and directness; about our own need to change and to be transformed if we were to be agents of Christ's peace.

CHAPTER 8

CORRYMEELA AND THE WIDER OUTREACH

'The Holy Spirit is that power which opens eyes that are closed, hearts that are unaware and minds that shrink from too much reality. If one is open towards God, one is open also to the beauty of the world, the truth of ideas, and the pain of disappointment and deformity. If one is closed up against being hurt, or blind towards one's brothers and sisters, one is inevitably shut off from God also. One cannot choose to be open in one direction and closed in another. Vision and vulnerability go together. Insensitivity also is an all-rounder. If for one reason or another we refuse to see another person we become incapable of sensing the presence of God. The Spirit of humanity is that facility which enables each of us to be truly present to another. The Spirit of God is that power of communion which enables every other reality, and God who is within and behind all realities, to be present to us.'

John V Taylor
The Go-Between God
(SCM Press 1972)

The physical dominance of the Corrymeela Centre at Ballycastle has sometimes put many other aspects of the life and work of the Community into the shade. However, as Leader I was given the task of holding together the work of our Centres with the rooted witness of members and friends in their own situations. Many of our members were living in circumstances where they were often lonely and isolated from sympathetic support. Although many of them continued to meet in small local cell groups, they often felt discouraged by the lack of priority given to peacemaking in their local churches. Those who were teachers often found themselves without the sympathetic support of their peers. Those involved in youth and community work lived with constant fears and dangers due to the ongoing violence. A few who were actively involved in politics were threatened at times by paramilitary groups.

I remember in particular visiting one member who lived close to an RUC barracks in West Belfast. The IRA had made several attempts to blow up the barracks but those who suffered most were in the houses nearby that took the full blast of the explosions. In this particular house the stairs had almost fallen down and much of the internal plaster was cracked and broken. A member of the Community, a single parent, sat on the damaged couch reading bedtime stories to her children and wondering when the next blast would come. During the difficult days of the 80s many of our members needed support and prayers if they were not to sink into despair. Mixed marriage couples were vulnerable to sectarian attacks as 'soft targets'. Those involved in local peace initiatives were sometimes threatened or intimidated. I received a number of hostile letters but was never personally attacked.

The anti-ecumenical stance of many in the Presbyterian Church was a matter of deep sadness and pain for myself and many of our members. Nevertheless, some of us felt it all the more necessary to make our witness there, and eventually this led to a recognition of peacemaking as a central part of our calling. Although an impressive statement of our commitment to peace and reconciliation was passed by the General Assembly, the process of following this up at congregational level was strongly resisted in many places. Sadly, for many, peace had become associated with surrender. The only peace they could accept was the peace of victory over the IRA. Slowly and very reluctantly many have come to see that compromise is necessary but it will be a long time before some can recognise that there was something deeply flawed in the society that existed before the Troubles.

However, many small initiatives did emerge, leading to dialogue and co-operation between congregations in Belfast, Lisburn, Kilrea and other places. The special relationship between Fitzroy Presbyterian Church and Clonard Monastery was one outstanding example of this and it has led to many significant relationships. Rev Ken Newell and Fr Gerry Reynolds gave strong leadership here and William Rutherford, a member of the Community and a casualty surgeon in the Royal Victoria Hospital, Belfast, was especially active in this initiative. William was also in a strategic role in the RVH at a time when that hospital was receiving casualties from every section of the community. Some of the leading players in the conflict were attended by him and his staff and their availability in times of crises at all hours was a symbol of the deep humanity which was shown by hospital staff in the midst of brutal violence.

Issues of justice and human rights were regularly being raised during this period. The Castlereagh Interrogation Centre had become notorious as a result of reports by Amnesty International. The police were, of course, in a very difficult situation with intense pressure on them to prevent or defeat terrorism. Courts were unable to use juries because of problems of intimidation in the case of scheduled offences (i.e. those related directly to the Troubles). The hunger strikes had raised issues about the treatment of prisoners and matters such as 'strip searching', especially in the case of women, were hotly debated. Together with Peter Tennant, a Quaker member of the Community and Peter McLachlan, Director of Bryson House, I became involved in a project to see how complaints against the police could be dealt with fairly and objectively. This work led us into contact with other groups working in the same field, including some academic lawyers and some members of the Community of the Peace People.

Eventually this resulted in the formation of the 'Committee for Administration of Justice'. Over the years this group has developed into the main human rights NGO in Northern Ireland and has acted as a watchdog and advocate of many structural changes. Although I have remained an active supporter of the CAJ, I have some concerns about the dangers of a purely 'rights based' culture unless it is complemented by a spirit of community and a commitment to the 'common good'. Nevertheless, the erosion of basic human rights has been one of the sad results of our conflict at times and any witness for peace must involve the exposure of this, whatever the source. I often found myself phoning the Police Interrogation Centre in order to find out if a person was being detained there and to ask for information on behalf of relatives. Discrimination in employment too has been a scourge in our society and a direct result of the sectarian attitudes that infect us all. Thankfully it is now largely outlawed, but the attitudes that produced it are far from changed yet.

Of the many specific situations in which I became involved in this sphere, one stands out. This was related to the case of the UDR4 – four soldiers who were challenging their conviction based on an alleged conspiracy leading to a murder of a republican in Armagh. I had taken a superficial interest in this case and had agreed to support a call for an appeal to be considered if the evidence was forthcoming (through a resolution passed at the Corrymeela Community AGM). It was only when I received a letter from one of the prisoners, Jim Hegan, that my mind was concentrated. The tone of the letter, and further letters that I agreed to receive, convinced me that I was dealing with an innocent man. Subsequently I went to visit him in prison and my earlier impressions were further confirmed. To cut a long story short, I became involved in a lengthy process, together with the parents of one of the soldiers, distinguished historian Robert Kee, members of the Church and Government Committee of the Presbyterian Church in Ireland and Mairéad Maguire, one of the Nobel Peace Prize winners. After a very long time, evidence was finally introduced to show that the confessions of the soldiers had been interfered with and supplemented at various points by the detectives. I tell this story not because it is especially significant but because it was a salutary experience of the dangers of miscarriages of justice unless we are truly vigilant. At the root of so much of our troubles there has been a blindness to injustices around us and a tendency to avoid involvement or to turn a blind eye. Truly the price of any real democracy is eternal vigilance. (Other members of Community have been involved in similar cases.)

Ballycastle itself was not immune from the troubles, although in comparison to other towns it was relatively peaceful. One serious incident which affected us all deeply was the murder of a young policeman whose family had close connections with the town. The local Corrymeela cell group played an important role in facilitating an interdenominational service in the car park where the murder had been committed. This proved to be a very healing occasion for all and helped to avoid a possible polarisation of attitudes in the town.

One of those convicted for involvement in this murder was Stephen Hill, some of whose close relatives were members of our staff. This was a difficult and painful time for them because they were equally as shocked as others to discover that he had been involved. I visited him in prison and went to court to ask for him to be given compassionate leave to attend his father's funeral. To my amazement I was entrusted with his care for the whole of the day without any policeman with me. Perhaps I am being naïve here and that we were in fact being closely monitored?

During these years we were also faced with many calls for help from individuals and families suffering from intimidation. The Community of the Peace People were heavily involved in this work at one stage and I often liaised with Pat Hale, who had made special arrangements for those who needed to leave the country. Corrymeela was sometimes asked to give temporary sanctuary to families and individuals until other possibilities of housing were made available. It wasn't always easy to distinguish between authentic examples of intimidation and others which, to say the least, were ambiguous. On several occasions I became aware that the families to which we extended sanctuary had themselves been involved in intimidating their neighbours, and in some case were the chief culprits! At times our policy of being open to all was sorely tested and we depended on our community workers and other contacts to try to assess each situation as carefully and compassionately as possible.

I have referred above to Peter Tennant who, with Valerie his wife, appeared on the scene at the beginning of my period of leadership. Peter had asked if there was any way in which he could become involved in the community. Ann Grant (a Community member who was also a Quaker) had encouraged him to meet some of us and he eventually became a deeply committed member. One story which has been told is that he observed me washing the windows of our Belfast Centre and concluded that a community in which the Leader washed the windows was worth joining. Little did he know how extremely rare an event he had witnessed!

In addition to planting thousands of trees at our Ballycastle Centre, and deep involvement with the Committee for Administration of Justice, Peter and

Valerie established a home on the slopes of Knocklayd and eventually built an annexe beside it for use by groups or individuals. Over the years this became a wonderful resource for volunteers, staff and Community members. When Peter and Valerie became too frail to remain there, the Community inherited the house and annexe and have developed it as a 'place apart' for small groups and individuals. With the help of Resident Volunteers, it has served the needs of the community and wider groups as a place for small retreats, bereavement support, training and dialogue etc. The generosity of Peter and Valerie to so many people during their 15 years in Ireland has left a deep impression on us all. It is but one example amongst many of the contribution of Quakers to the healing of wounds in these islands. Knocklayd can complement the Ballycastle Centre in many ways with its more restful ethos and space for nurturing the spiritual roots of our life. Some members feel that this is especially necessary at this stage on our journey.

Many of the wider activities of Corrymeela were simply enjoyable and involved social and musical events and opportunities to travel and make friends all over the world. The Corrymeela Singers were founded and led by Norman Richardson in the mid-70s. They have continued to be an active group within the life of the Community. Shirley and I enjoyed our involvement with them over many years. It enabled us to get to know members and friends in a relaxed setting. In addition to that, the Singers contributed to many special occasions in the life of Corrymeela. These included the Annual Dedication Services in January, Summerfest, broadcast services and the special Corrymeela Sunday occasions all over Britain. Many of these occasions were opportunities to be roving ambassadors for the vision and message of the Community. Very often this has given us access to local churches in Ireland and we have supported many outreach projects such as Christian Aid, as well as our own work.

One of the joys of the Singers has been the opportunity it provided for members to write their own music and compose songs which reflected some of the themes of peace, reconciliation, suffering and healing. Norman Richardson's musical settings and original compositions are still regularly performed. Roger Courtney's song 'The Pollen of Peace' is now widely known. Janet Shepperson, Jacynth Hamill and others have contributed songs and music. It was a deeply moving experience to sing Janet's song, 'One Small Candle' in the presence of Pope John Paul II at the Olympic Stadium in Vienna before 60,000 people. It wasn't always easy to agree on the most suitable repertoire for the group and some members of Community were not impressed by our musical style at times. We have had a succession of musical directors since Norman stepped aside and we remember with gratitude the contributions of Jill McLachlan, Barbara Jennings, John Chilvers and Rowena Eames.

The mention of 'Corrymeela Sunday' brings to mind the close co-operation that I had with the Corrymeela Link – our support group based in Reading, but with a network of small cells all over Britain. The continuous support of this group, in terms of prayer, education and finance, has been an ongoing miracle that was sustained through the difficult years of the Troubles. The staff and committee at Reading showed a loyalty and dedication to our cause, without which our activities would have been seriously reduced. It was my privilege to be the main ambassador for the work of the Community for a period, and through the Link I was given access to local groups throughout the length and breadth of Britain. The Link followed in the footsteps of earlier initiatives by Coventry Cathedral that had led to the building of a special house for our volunteers and staff (Coventry House) and the London Corrymeela Venture.

Corrymeela Sunday occasions, held on the Sunday closest to St Patrick's Day, often included a full weekend of activities. A youth group from Northern Ireland would meet up with local youth, and the Corrymeela Singers and a team of speakers would usually be involved. Some very humorous incidents took place at times and I particularly remember an incident at Liverpool Catholic Cathedral (Paddy's Wigwam). Our youth group was preparing to rehearse a mime that was to take place at the service. They arrived at the Cathedral carrying a series of posters with all the grafitti that accompanies sectarian parades in Northern Ireland. Phrases such as 'BRITS OUT', 'NO POPE HERE' and many others were vividly displayed on the posters. A Euro MP about to attend the service spotted the group walking towards the cathedral. Thinking that they might be a group wishing to disrupt the service, she phoned the police and had the young people arrested. We had great difficulty getting them released in time to perform their mime in the cathedral!

Support for our work came from a wide variety of places all over the world and this required me to make occasional visits to give feedback to our supporters and to give them a real feeling of belonging to our movement. In some instances this involved dealing with many of the myths and distortions of our situation and countering support for violence emanating from parts of the United States. But some of our most faithful support groups were also from the US and the opportunity to meet many of them and thank them for their encouragement led to many new friendships. German support groups were also very significant during the 80s and we were often asked to share with them in projecting our work at the massive Kirchentags during those years. The development of special links with the Swedish Lutheran Centre at Stiffsgarten, Rattvik, during this period was another enriching relationship leading to regular two-way visits by many of our young adults. During the period when the Berlin Wall was in place, our youth workers made special use of exchanges there to open up reflection on 'Divided Societies' and to widen the perspectives of young people who had never been out of Northern Ireland.

One of the tensions which tends to occur within Corrymeela, especially since the programme and other staff numbers have grown, is in the relationships between staff, long term volunteers and community members. The Community have always been concerned to maintain a close partnership here and to avoid any sense that they simply paid the staff to work on their behalf. In order to facilitate this members have been encouraged to give some to voluntary work and 'presence' at our centres, and staff and volunteers have been encouraged to spend some time away from the centres in order to understand local contexts.

Because Community members think of the Ballycastle Centre as their 'home' there is always a danger that they can forget that for many of the staff and volunteers it is their permanent place of life and work. Members' weekends can feel like a 'takeover bid' unless due sensitivity is shown. It is equally dangerous when staff become so preoccupied with their own agenda that they cease to understand the needs of members who are trying to live out their commitment often in lonely and difficult situations.

This tension is potentially a creative one through which we can all gain support and enrichment from one another, but unless it is worked at it can become destructive. Staff have often experienced a lack of awareness from members of the stress and tension of their work, and have felt very unsupported on some occasions. Members have sometimes felt that too much emphasis has been given to the work of our Centres and too little to support for the wider witness of members and friends in their local situations. If Corrymeela is to be a bridge and not an island, this wider outreach must be nurtured, and if we ask for too much involvement of members at the Centres we will weaken their local involvements. However it would be equally damaging to lose the partnership with our staff. The best models of work have often arisen where local and centre contributions are complementary, e.g. in twinned church or school programmes. As some areas of staff work are becoming more specialised, this partnership is not always possible but sometimes the special skills required are found amongst members whose daily work is in the areas of mediation, trauma counselling, etc. Corrymeela is above all else about the nurturing of relationships and this is facilitated in many different settings through Council, committees, cell groups, etc., but it does require time and patience.

Another not unrelated subject currently under discussion is the optimum size of the Community and the staff. To put an arbitrary figure such as 250 on our membership may result in a hidden pressure on older less physically active members to transfer to the 'Friends' list in order to make more room for youth. It could also discourage those who live at some distance (e.g. South Africa or France) from maintaining their membership because they cannot be physically present on enough occasions. Some feel that the Community would be greatly impoverished by the loss of such people. Some feel that the essential aspect of membership is the shared vision and commitment and that can be even more important to those who are feeling isolated or live far away. Also the contribution of older members and their need for continued support should not be underestimated. I well remember an occasion when a volunteer asked what was the point of a certain member, who was beginning to look a bit decrepit, remaining within the Community. I realised at once that the young person had no knowledge of the life and witness of that person and had not yet had the chance to draw from the hidden treasures of wisdom and experience which were to be found there.

The new category of 'Associate' may offer a possibility for some who find it difficult to fulfil the current commitment but would like to retain some deeper sense of belonging which is not offered under the category of 'Friend'. The 5-6000 Friends vary greatly, from those who have been long standing supporters, some more active at times than members, and those who have only a very limited connection. Whatever we decide I am sure that there will always be some blurred lines here as people's circumstances change from year to year.

When the Community was founded in 1965, the original group did not envisage that we would be so preoccupied with reconciliation in Northern Ireland. Part of our earlier vision was about the renewal of the church, the nature of Christian community, the vocation of lay people in the world and the wider issues of world peace and social change. Hopefully, if the peace process progresses, we will be able to give more priority to some of those earlier agendas and some new ones as well such as 'caring for creation'. Issues such as the partnership of men and women, the challenge of hospitality for economic refugees and our relations with other faiths, are already assuming greater importance and they are all dimensions of reconciliation.

However, it is unlikely that the tasks of peacemaking in Ireland will be significantly reduced in the immediate future. In the current period of transition, sectarianism has expressed itself even more ferociously and it still has the potential to poison all the achievements of recent years. The loyalist perception that their culture is in the process of being annihilated can produce a very defensive approach to the peace process. Suppressed pain due to past trauma is now being more keenly felt, and the spirit of repentance, healing and forgiveness is still in short supply. A long and painful journey still awaits us as we seek to bring about a society where everyone can feel that they belong and where diversity is celebrated or at least respected.

We will need to draw more deeply on our spiritual resources if we are to find the energy and commitment to continue on this journey. How easy it is for any of us to fall back into the pattern of choosing only to be with those with whom we feel comfortable and avoiding those who are difficult or different. Jean Vanier has taught us that it is only as we acknowledge our vulnerability that we can become open to receive each other's gifts and in the process meet Christ afresh. As a Community we are no more immune from the breakdown of relationships than the wider church and society. Some of our members have experienced divorce and separation and we have no magic formulae for resolving these situations. Very slowly we have learnt to support each other and to give space for the sharing of our vulnerability. We can grow and learn through pain, but when that doesn't happen we can be emotionally crippled and end up perpetual victims. We have seen how all of life can be 'grist to the mill' when the bereaved or ex-prisoners come through painful experiences and, by the grace of God, emerge as fuller and more human persons. A well-known poster often on sale at Corrymeela illustrates this philosophy graphically: It depicts a caterpillar crawling along the leaf of a tree. The caption below says, 'Please be patient, God is not finished with me yet.' It is the conviction that God does not give up on us, so all the experiences of life can be part of our reshaping, if only we are open enough to allow it to happen.

Life in the Community has often bound us together closely as we tried to maintain a witness and be a sign of hope for our divided society. A number of members and former members have died and it was often at such times that we became most conscious, not only of our deep sense of loss, but also of a deep sense of gratitude for the gifts that we had received from those with whom we had shared so many experiences. Perhaps this was most poignant in 1978 when Billy McAllister died. Billy had been the embodiment of Corrymeela since the Centre was purchased and had been a one-man general factotum as warden, work camp organiser and amateur philosopher from 1965-78. He had welded together hundreds of young volunteers and imbued them with the spirit of Corrymeela. When he joined us he had just retired from work with the Great Northern Railway, but for the next thirteen years he had a new lease of life. Mind you, his enterprising spirit could create embarrassment at times, as on the occasion when he decided to demolish a building without even consulting the Centre Director (Harold Good).

Donald McDonagh, a schoolteacher at Coleraine Inst, died in the early 80s. He had been one of the early members of the Community and a tower of strength in shaping its spirit and ethos. His loss after a lengthy illness was palpable because he had seemed to be at the fullness of his powers. His wife, Isobel, continues to be active and involved in every aspect of our life today. The sudden death of Joe Harris was a shock to us all and the deaths of Frank Wright and Roel Kaptein were particularly poignant for me. I mention the above because of my very close association and personal friendship with them and not to imply that those I have not named were any the less valued or missed. Indeed other deaths of young people with whom we had worked through suicide, accident or terrorism were equally traumatic. And yet, in all these occasions, they also had the effect of binding us together more deeply as a Community.

During this period, our own family life was passing through significant stages. Duncan, our eldest son, went to Oxford in 1979; Philip to Canterbury a year later; Alison to Edinburgh in 1982 and Neil to Sheffield in 1986. Shirley's twin brother, who lived in London, became seriously ill and this necessitated frequent visits and times of support and care until he died in 1987. This period was one of great strain for us both and it was difficult to balance all the needs of family with other pressures. My father had died in 1979 after a short illness but my mother became increasingly confused with the onset of Alzheimer's Disease. My weekly visits to the nursing home were nevertheless an important part of my own personal journey through experiencing the harsh realities of this kind of death.

During this whole period I was greatly supported by my predecessor and our founder, Ray Davey and Kathleen his wife. At no time did they create any difficulties for me, even when I made decisions that were probably faulty. They were there for me in a supportive and encouraging way and remained available to fill many of the gaps that had to be filled, often at very short notice. Indeed Ray's contribution to the life and work of the Community was in many ways every bit as significant during this time as it was when he was full-time leader. His regular presence at the Centre, contributions to new volunteers and members, his books and articles and wider work as our most valuable ambassador and his unobtrusive presence, as friend to all, was a precious gift indeed. Kathleen's contribution was equally significant and in all sorts of ways she was an active presence and friend to all.

CHAPTER 9

THE PEACE PROCESS
FAITH, POLITICS & RECONCILIATION

Easter Rising 1998:

The Suffering,
lead heavy,
begins to lift
despite
the sorrow,
deep as mines,
and acid hate
now dissolving
in necessary compromise.

Today
hope walked again
in Belfast squares
as bells in the steeples
of Ulster's history
rang our Easter chimes.

Here were held
in combat
death and resurrection,
expectancy and despair,
love and anger;
joy was iced with pain
as the past
began to unfreeze
and optimism gained
a footing
on the slopes of faith.

Still standing
by the Cross on its hill
as these last
two thousand years
when other disciples ran away
were a few solitary women,
Northern Ireland's
prophets of re-generation.'

Brian Frost

In 1990 Colin Craig was appointed Centre Director at Corrymeela, Ballycastle and he took up his post in the Autumn. Colin had applied for the post in 1985 when Michael Earle was appointed, so it was very courageous of him to put his head on the chopping block a second time. He had been a member of the Community for many years and had a lot of experience in work with young adult offenders. He was also a world-class canoeist and very committed to using the physical resources of the Ballycastle region in some of our programmes for building relationships, trust and co-operation.

It was becoming clear to me that my energy level was fading a bit, so I decided to ask for a Sabbatical break but with the additional request that the Community begin the process of looking for a future leader. Colin brought some new energy to the task of Centre Director and, together with Rachel his wife, they were soon taking hold of the direction and development of the work at the Centre. He did have some difficulty at first letting go of work linked with his previous post but he soon realised that this job left little room for extras.

During this period, John Hume, the leader of the SDLP, had taken the decision to open talks with Gerry Adams, leader of Sinn Féin. This was regarded as very controversial, not only by Unionists (who believed that Sinn Féin were indistinguishable from the IRA and that negotiations with 'Terrorists' were wrong and always counterproductive) but also by many members of his own party. Many people felt that this move was making it impossible to achieve political progress between constitutional parties and some saw it as the beginning of a pan-Nationalist movement to push for British withdrawal from Northern Ireland.

In retrospect we can now see that John Hume believed that it was possible to convince the Sinn Féin leader that Britain had no selfish, strategic or economic interest in remaining in Ireland, but was simply committed to the principle of 'consent'. On this basis he hoped to persuade Sinn Féin to call a ceasefire and to take part in talks aimed to find a structure of government that gave full recognition to both Irish and British traditions. Hume wanted a totally inclusive process of talks because he believed that excluding the whole republican tradition would not bring about a lasting peace. It is now clear that he was also aware that the IRA did not want to continue the armed struggle and was open to some face-saving way of moving into constitutional politics.

The many twists and turns of that process have gone on for ten years now, but although we have not yet got a fully stable agreement we have come a long way, and to my mind it would be tragic to turn back at this stage. Many small initiatives by groups and individuals during this period contributed to the climate that gave voice to the deep desire for peace from many grassroots groups. On the other hand, many others, mainly from the Unionist tradition, believe that the peace process was a 'surrender' process from the time that Sinn Féin was allowed to take part.

One project with which I was closely involved was Initiative '92. This was the brainchild of Simon Lee, a law lecturer at QUB, and Robin Wilson, editor of *Fortnight* magazine. In an attempt to fill the vacuum caused by the lack of political progress, this initiative invited groups from every section of society to make submissions regarding the way forward in relation to social, economic and political issues of public concern. Torkel Opsahl, a Norwegian human rights lawyer, acted as the chairperson of a panel of people from within and outside Northern Ireland. Many of the submissions were presented at public hearings in different parts of the country. The Opsahl Report attempted to summarise some of the key recommendations and a committee was appointed to follow through the proposals with schools, community groups, churches and politicians.

Most politicians were wary of this effort, perhaps because they felt that it was invading their pitch, but they could not ignore the effects of it, empowering many people to put pressure on them to be more constructive. At a time when there was a danger of the public drifting into a sense of hopeless apathy, it did generate some momentum and political education. Corrymeela Current Affairs Group made a submission, largely drafted by Duncan Morrow, and it is interesting in retrospect to note some of the points made there:

We began by stating that 'attempts to develop or impose political structures on Northern Ireland which deny the reality that one part of the population is hostile to the British State while another is hostile to an all-Ireland state will always founder on the rock of sociological and empirical fact.' With regard to the Anglo-Irish Agreement we said two key aspects of it should be retained: (1) 'The recognition at international level of the dual or bi-national reality of Northern Ireland.' (2) 'The obligation on both the United Kingdom and the Republic of Ireland to work together.' We went on to say that 'settlement in Northern Ireland will require real institutional changes in the relationship of the Irish Republic and the United Kingdom. Both will have to accept the involvement of the other in each other's affairs for the foreseeable future'; 'North-South relations should be promoted at all levels; (but) to prevent unionists seeing this as dealing with the problem only in an Irish context rather than one which involves Irish nationalists' equally difficult relations with Britain, the '"triangular' structure Britain – Ireland – Northern Ireland", will have to be maintained in all things, including cultural exchange.'

With regard to policing we said that 'only when there is an internal structure of government in Northern Ireland which can command the loyalty of nationalists will it be possible to recruit nationalists to the police in numbers commensurate with their share of the population.' Finally, we stressed that 'Whatever formal structures are agreed there will be a continued need for models of trust at all levels of society from top to bottom.'

Corrymeela's interest in reflecting on social and political issues from within a 'faith perspective' has been an important part of our work over the years and the above statement grows out of such reflection. The 'Faith and Politics

Group' that began in 1983 with the support of Corrymeela, Irish School of Ecumenics and Glencree Centre for Reconciliation, had been producing pamphlets for reflection and action for members of churches and those active in politics. These covered topics like the Anglo-Irish Agreement, *Political Funerals, Remembering our Past, Towards an Ireland that Works* and many of the issues arising in the peace process. These included the painful issue of the early release of prisoners, the meaning of parity of esteem, forgiveness and the tasks of peacemaking.

Fr Brian Lennon, a Jesuit priest, played a very active part as secretary of this group, and amongst Corrymeela members who made a major contribution, David Stevens was outstanding in the role of drafting many of the pamphlets. As a group representing Protestants and Catholics in both the North and the South of Ireland, we were concerned to reflect together on the social and political issues of our time and seek to discern what Christian obedience required of us. Because of our history, we were concerned to avoid any over-identification with Unionism or Nationalism, to be self-critical where it was necessary and to seek to stimulate reflection throughout our churches, political parties and governments – British and Irish. We also arranged many meetings with leading members of political parties, the police, Orange Order, church leaders and church groups in order to understand their viewpoints and to debate our pamphlets. It was an important part of our peace witness.

Following a Sabbatical break in 1992, which Shirley and I spent in New Zealand and Australia, Trevor Williams was appointed to the leadership of Corrymeela and took up his post in March 1993. Trevor and his wife Joyce had been members of the Community for a number of years and Trevor brought to the leadership many gifts. He had much experience in the field of media communication as a result of many years work with the BBC. He was also an experienced Church of Ireland pastor with training in counselling. Having lived in both South and the North of Ireland he had a good awareness of the many differing perspectives that the tasks of reconciliation has to address. We have all been greatly blessed by his leadership since his appointment.

I took up the post of Northern Ireland lecturer and NI co-ordinator of the

Irish School of Ecumenics at this time, working under the supervision of Alan Falconer, the Director of the School. My work was largely based in the North and involved taking over the courses that had been run for some time by Fr Michael Hurley SJ (the founder of the Irish School of Ecumenics) and developing the adult education aspect of the work in different parts of the country. During this time, after Alan Falconer was called to work with the World Council of Churches in Geneva, Geraldine Smyth OP was appointed Director of the School. This led to the setting up of a major research project based in Belfast on the theme of 'Moving Beyond Sectarianism'.

The two people appointed to carry through this work under Geraldine's supervision were Cecelia Clegg, a sister of La Retraite, and Joe Leichty, an American Mennonite who had been researching Irish history for some time. My task was to help the group establish a wide spectrum of contacts with both traditions here as a base for their research. The full results of this 5-year project have just been published and it is hoped that it will be of real value to all our churches. The task of acknowledging and owning sectarianism is the first step in a journey by which we can begin to transcend it and truly be an agent of reconciliation in our society.

One other encouragement of this period was the emergence of the Evangelical Contribution on Northern Ireland (ECONI). Because of the strong anti-ecumenical atmosphere in Northern Ireland, further aggravated by the Troubles, many evangelicals were wary of close involvement with Roman Catholics and of groups like Corrymeela. A Declaration of Faith and Commitment, produced by the Faith and Politics Group after the Anglo Irish Agreement, was signed by some evangelicals, but others felt that something different was needed if it was to touch their constituency. Under the leadership of David Porter, this group has emerged to challenge all those within the evangelical tradition to take on board the gospel imperative to peacemaking. By targeting their efforts directly at a specific constituency, they have been able to awaken a significant response and self-critique from many, including some significant leaders within Unionism. They have now become important partners in peacemaking with many other groups and their sharp and courageous thinking has influenced us all.

They have drawn their inspiration from many sources but one important source has been the US Mennonites. This Anabaptist group with strong biblical roots and a strong peacemaking tradition has influenced many other groups in recent years, not least in the area of mediation. Unlike some American groups, they have come amongst us in great humility and have won the trust of many by their unobtrusive presence.

The 'peace process', as it has come to be called since the ceasefires of the mid-90s, has been a fragile plant from its beginning and it remains so even to this day. Nevertheless, we have come a long way and it is hard to believe that we could squander all the gains of these past years, in spite of the problems that remain to be solved.

New relationships have developed as a result of much dialogue and friendship with members of Sinn Féin, some former paramilitary leaders from both Loyalist and Republican traditions. The work of several priests from Clonard Monastery was of immense help in bridging some of these gulfs and keeping channels of communication alive when trust had broken down. In learning to recognise each other's humanity we began to break out of our harsh stereotyping of one another. The crucial role of Senator George Mitchell has been recognised widely, as he modelled the work of listening with patience and long suffering. Slowly and gradually the architecture of war and conflict has begun to be dismantled and a more normal life has become possible for us all.

But the work of reconciliation has only begun. War weariness, rather than full-blooded commitment to a new vision of society, is the norm. The legacy of our troubles is one of deep wounds that remain largely unhealed at this stage. The process of transition from conflict to a more genuinely peaceful society is going to be a long and painful journey. Many are still nostalgic and grieving for a society that they have lost. They cannot see a constructive future for their tradition. The Orange Order is perhaps most symbolic of this sense of pain and lostness, but it is widespread in the Loyalist community. Even Republicans and Nationalists who look more positively at the peace process, have not yet come to terms with the difficult compromises that it requires. Many do not realise how the Republic of Ireland has moved on and that the older style of nationalism has been outmoded. Many Unionists are still totally unaware of the changing concept of 'Britishness' that is emerging in an increasingly multi-cultural society on the other island.

There is a danger that our churches and other institutions will continue to reinforce a benign apartheid by opting out of all initiatives to cross the divide and by concentrating exclusively on maintaining their own structures. The sectarian structures in our society are systemic and unless their boundaries become open to a two-way flow an unstable society will continue. In that situation only an occasional act can fuel communal violence once again. Obedience to Christ requires the courage to cross these old boundaries.

Nevertheless it is a time of great opportunity for the ongoing witness for reconciliation. The economic regeneration, which we see all around us, is welcome because it provides jobs for so many people whose past opportunities have been frustrated by unemployment and discrimination. But we know that we are part of Western affluent consumer society and part of the problem of an unsustainable world economy. Unless our peacemaking is part of that indivisible peace of our planet and world society, it will be illusory. Yet we can give thanks for so much received on a bumpy journey and feel some excitement in the knowledge that the journey continues and Jesus leads us on into ever new paths and in unexpected ways.

On this journey we have learnt that the concept of reconciliation has sometimes been devalued and used in superficial ways. It has therefore been dismissed by some as papering over the cracks and accused of failing to face up to the deep injustices which need to be removed if real healing is to take place. It can be reduced to 'cheap grace' as if saying sorry is enough to release people from further moral obligations. However, any fair examination of the New Testament shows that such a reduction of the concept is a distortion of its meaning.

At the heart of the New Testament understanding is the conviction that in the life, death and resurrection of Jesus Christ an act of cosmic healing took place: 'God was in Christ reconciling the world to Himself.' It was a Divine initiative overcoming the alienation and hostility between God, humanity and all creation. This has opened up a way of entering into a new reconciled relationship with God, with one another because we discover that the alienation and hostility has been broken down, and with creation as we learn how to receive it afresh as a gift rather than a possession. This action of God is not simply a possibility, it is an event which we proclaim as good news for all, although we can only enter into it through the gift of the Spirit.

There are four key elements involved if it is to be a truly transformative process. These are: forgiveness, repentance, truth and justice. If any of these are neglected we end up with cheap grace. The process can be initiated by the victim or the perpetrator (although in many conflict situations we are both) and nothing happens without risk and vulnerability. Attempts to give justice the priority can sometimes be counterproductive, because without some relationship which makes listening possible it is not possible to seek justice or know what it might mean. Oppressed groups can quickly become oppressors unless there is a transformation in the relationship which enables all parties to envisage a mutually enriching future. An essential part of the process of reconciliation is the felt need of people to tell their stories or to hear the stories of others. The Truth and Reconciliation Commission in South Africa has shown how deeply people feel the need to hear the truth about what happened to their loved ones. But truth alone cannot prevent rivalry about whose story is to triumph, so without forgiveness it can become another weapon in the fight to claim who is the greatest victim. Forgiveness itself can never be commanded, it is often a lengthy process with many stages and it is always a kind of miracle when it happens. But even when forgiveness has been offered, it cannot be received without repentance if reconciliation is to happen.

There is no simple ordering of these dimensions which can apply to all situations, but if any of them is missing the healing process will be limited if not blocked. It is, of course, always more complex to apply them to communities as well as individuals, to Protestant and Catholic communities and to British and Irish nations, but they do apply nevertheless. We can be thankful for all the small initiatives over the past few years which have moved the process forward in spite of many set backs. 'It's better to light ten candles even if nine blow out.' We know that the journey has barely started for many. Only the conviction that we belong together, a willingness to take risks and a growing vision of a new and common future in which diversity is respected can motivate the process. A new future is being offered to us if only we have the grace to enter into it.

POSTSCRIPT

Since completing the script of this memoir there has been a very unstable period in community relations and in the Political Process. Sections of the Loyalist paramilitaries (especially the Ulster Defence Force and the Loyalist Volunteer Force) have been active in violence, using pipe bombs and blast bombs to intimidate and sometimes kill Catholics. Republican dissidents have also been active in disrupting trains and targeting security forces, etc. In North Belfast in particular there has been widespread community tension, often orchestrated by paramilitaries, and the police have paid a heavy price in attempting to keep the peace. Police morale is low because of the changes being introduced as a result of the Patten Report. However, the recent breakthrough allowing the setting up of a new Police Board with representation from moderate Nationalism (SDLP) gives hope for the development of policing with consent. The deep-seated fear of change in Loyalist working class areas continues to be a major obstacle to the creation of community peace.

The Political Process reached crisis point in the early summer due to the failure of the IRA to begin decommissioning. A breakthrough was achieved in October which has the potential to breathe new life into the process. The changed global atmosphere in the wake of the 11 September events in the United States has undoubtedly put pressure on all paramilitary organisations to make progress in disarmament. Nevertheless the transition from a war zone to a more peaceful society will continue to be painful and frustrating. The reality of our commitment to 'seek peace and pursue it' will continue to test us to the full. I pray that we will not become weary in well-doing so 'that in due time we can reap a reward'.

JWM November 2001